CHATEAU AND COUNTRY LIFE IN FRANCE

LECTOR HOUSE PUBLIC DOMAIN WORKS

CHATEAU AND COUNTRY LIFE IN FRANCE

MARY KING WADDINGTON

ISBN: 978-93-5614-704-1

Published: 1909

LECTOR HOUSE LLP
E-MAIL: info@lectorhouse.com

A country wedding

CHATEAU AND COUNTRY LIFE IN FRANCE

BY

MARY KING WADDINGTON

AUTHOR OF LETTERS OF A DIPLOMAT'S WIFE AND ITALIAN LETTERS OF A DIPLOMAT'S WIFE

ILLUSTRATED

1909

CONTENTS

LIST OF ILLUSTRATIONS

A fine old château.

I

CHATEAU LIFE

My first experience of country life in France, about thirty years ago, was in a fine old château standing high in pretty, undulating, wooded country close to the forest of Villers-Cotterets, and overlooking the great plains of the Oise—big green fields stretching away to the sky-line, broken occasionally by little clumps of wood, with steeples rising out of the green, marking the villages and hamlets which, at intervals, are scattered over the plains, and in the distance the blue line of the forest. The château was a long, perfectly simple, white stone building. When I first saw it, one bright November afternoon, I said to my husband as we drove up, "What a charming old wooden house!" which remark so astonished him that he could hardly explain that it was all stone, and that no big houses (nor small, either) in France were built of wood. I, having been born in a large white wooden house in America, couldn't understand why he was so horrified at my ignorance of French architecture. It was a fine old house, high in the centre, with a lower wing on each side. There were three drawing-rooms, a library, billiard-room, and dining-room on the ground floor. The large drawing-room, where we always sat, ran straight through the house, with glass doors opening out on the lawn on the entrance side and on the other into a long gallery which ran almost the whole length of the house. It was always filled with plants and flowers, open in summer, with awnings to keep out the sun; shut in winter with glass windows, and warmed by one of the three calorifères of the house. In front of the gallery the lawn sloped down to the wall, which separated the place from the highroad. A belt of fine trees marked the path along the wall and shut out the road completely, except in certain places where an opening had been made for the view.

We were a small party for such a big house: only the proprietor and his wife (old people), my husband and myself. The life was very simple, almost austere. The old people lived in the centre of the château, W.[1] and I in one of the wings. It had been all fitted up for us, and was a charming little house. W. had the ground-floor—a bedroom, dressing-room, cabinet de travail, dining-room, and a small room, half reception-room, half library, where he had a large bookcase filled with books, which he gave away as prizes or to school libraries. The choice of the books always interested me. They were principally translations, English and American—Walter Scott, Marryat, Fenimore Cooper, etc. The bedroom and cabinet de travail had glass doors opening on the park. I had the same rooms upstairs, giving one to

[1] W. here and throughout this volume refers to Mme. Waddington's husband, M. William Waddington.

my maid, for I was nervous at being so far away from anyone. M. and Mme. A. and all the servants were at the other end of the house, and there were no bells in our wing (nor anywhere else in the house except in the dining-room). When I wanted a work-woman who was sewing in the lingerie I had to go up a steep little winding staircase, which connected our wing with the main building, and walk the whole length of the gallery to the lingerie, which was at the extreme end of the other wing. I was very fond of my rooms. The bedroom and sitting-room opened on a balcony with a lovely view over wood and park. When I sat there in the morning with my petit déjeuner—cup of tea and roll—I could see all that went on in the place. First the keeper would appear, a tall, handsome man, rather the northern type, with fair hair and blue eyes, his gun always over his shoulder, sacoche at his side, swinging along with the free, vigorous step of a man accustomed to walk all day. Then Hubert, the coachman, would come for orders, two little fox-terriers always accompanying him, playing and barking, and rolling about on the grass. Then the farmer's wife, driving herself in her gig, and bringing cheese, butter, milk, and sometimes chickens when our bassecour was getting low. A little later another lot would appear, people from the village or canton, wanting to see their deputy and have all manner of grievances redressed. It was curious sometimes to make out, at the end of a long story, told in peasant dialect, with many digressions, what particular service notre député was expected to render. I was present sometimes at some of the conversations, and was astounded at W.'s patience and comprehension of what was wanted—I never understood half.

We generally had our day to ourselves. We rode almost every morning—long, delicious gallops in the woods, the horses going easily and lightly over the grass roads; and the days W. was away and couldn't ride, I used to walk about the park and gardens. The kitchen garden was enormous—almost a park in itself—and in the season I eat pounds of white grapes, which ripened to a fine gold color on the walls in the sun. We rarely saw M. and Mme. A. until twelve-o'clock breakfast.

Sometimes when it was fine we would take a walk with the old people after breakfast, but we generally spent our days apart. M. and Mme. A. were charming people, intelligent, cultivated, reading everything and keeping quite in touch with all the literary and Protestant world, but they had lived for years entirely in the country, seeing few people, and living for each other. The first evenings at the château made a great impression upon me. We dined at 7:30, and always sat after dinner in the big drawing-room. There was one lamp on a round table in the middle of the room (all the corners shrouded in darkness). M. and Mme. A. sat in two arm-chairs opposite to each other, Mme. A. with a green shade in front of her. Her eyes were very bad; she could neither read nor work. She had been a beautiful musician, and still played occasionally, by heart, the classics. I loved to hear her play Beethoven and Handel, such a delicate, old-fashioned touch. Music was at once a bond of union. I often sang for her, and she liked everything I sang—Italian stornelli, old-fashioned American negro songs, and even the very light modern French chansonnette, when there was any melody in them. There were two other arm-chairs at the table, destined for W. and me. I will say W. never occupied his. He would sit for about half an hour with M. A. and talk politics or local matters with him, but after that he departed to his own quarters, and I remained with the old people. I felt very strange at first, it was so unlike anything I had ever seen, so different from my home life, where we were a happy, noisy family, always one of the party, generally two, at the piano, everybody laughing, talking, and enjoying life, and always a troop of visitors, cousins innumerable and friends.

I loved to hear her play Beethoven and Handel.

It was a curious atmosphere. I can't say dull exactly, for both M. and Mme. A. were clever, and the discussions over books, politics, and life generally, were interesting, but it was serious, no vitality, nothing gay, no power of enjoyment. They had had a great grief in their lives in the loss of an only daughter,[2] which had left permanent traces. They were very kind and did their best to make me feel at home, and after the first few evenings I didn't mind. M. A. had always been in the habit

[2] W.'s first wife.

of reading aloud to his wife for an hour every evening after dinner—the paper, an article in one of the reviews, anything she liked. I liked that, too, and as I felt more at home used to discuss everything with M. A. He was quite horrified one evening when I said I didn't like Molière, didn't believe anybody did (particularly foreigners), unless they had been brought up to it.

It really rather worried him. He proposed to read aloud part of the principal plays, which he chose very carefully, and ended by making a regular cours de Molière. He read charmingly, with much spirit, bringing out every touch of humour and fancy, and I was obliged to say I found it most interesting. We read all sorts of things besides Molière—Lundis de Ste.-Beuve, Chateaubriand, some splendid pages on the French Revolution, Taine, Guizot, Mme. de Staël, Lamartine, etc., and sometimes rather light memoirs of the Régence and the light ladies of the eighteenth century, who apparently mixed up politics, religion, literature, and lovers in the most simple style. These last readings he always prepared beforehand, and I was often surprised at sudden transitions and unfinished conversations which meant that he had suppressed certain passages which he judged too improper for general reading.

He read, one evening, a charming feuilleton of George Sand. It began: "Le Baron avait causé politique toute la soirée," which conversation apparently so exasperated the baronne and a young cousin that they wandered out into the village, which they immediately set by the ears. The cousin was an excellent mimic of all animals' noises. He barked so loud and so viciously that he started all the dogs in the village, who went nearly mad with excitement, and frightened the inhabitants out of their wits. Every window was opened, the curé, the garde champêtre, the school-master, all peering out anxiously into the night, and asking what was happening. Was it tramps, or a travelling circus, or a bear escaped from his showman, or perhaps a wolf? I have wished sometimes since, when I have heard various barons talking politics, that I, too, could wander out into the night and seek distraction outside.

It was a serious life in the big château. There was no railway anywhere near, and very little traffic on the highroad. After nightfall a mantle of silence seemed to settle on the house and park—that absolute silence of great spaces where you almost hear your own heart beat. W. went to Paris occasionally, and usually came back by the last train, getting to the château at midnight. I always waited for him upstairs in my little salon, and the silence was so oppressive that the most ordinary noise—a branch blowing across a window-pane, or a piece of charred wood falling on the hearth—sounded like a cannon shot echoing through the long corridor. It was a relief when I heard the trot of his big mare at the top of the hill, quite fifteen minutes before he turned into the park gates. He has often told me how long and still the evenings and nights were during the Franco-Prussian War. He remained at the château all through the war with the old people. After Sedan almost the whole Prussian army passed the château on their way to Versailles and Paris. The big white house was seen from a long distance, so, as soon as it was dark, all the wooden shutters on the side of the highroad were shut, heavy curtains drawn, and strict orders given to have as little light as possible. He was sitting in his library one evening about dusk, waiting for the man to bring his lamp and shut the shutters, having had a trying day with the peasants, who were all frightened and nervous at the approach of the Germans. He was quite absorbed in rather melancholy reflections when he suddenly felt that someone was looking in at the window (the library was on the ground-floor, with doors and windows opening on the park). He rose quickly, going to the window, as he thought one of the village people wanted to speak to him, and was confronted by a Pickelhaube and a round German face flattened against the window-pane. He opened the window at once, and the man poured forth a torrent of German, which W. fortunately understood. While he was talking W. saw forms, their muskets and helmets showing out quite distinctly in the half-light, crossing the lawn and coming up some of the broad paths. It was a disagreeable sight, which he was destined to see many times.

It was wonderful what exact information the Germans had. They knew all the roads, all the villages and little hamlets, the big châteaux, and most of the small mills and farms. There were still traces of the German occupation when I went to that part of the country; on some of the walls and houses marks in red paint—"4 Pferde, 12 Männer." They generally wanted food and lodging, which they usually (not always) paid for. Wherever they found horses they took them, but M. A. and W. had sent all theirs away except one saddle-horse, which lived in a stable in the woods near the house. In Normandy, near Rouen, at my brother-in-law's place, they had German officers and soldiers quartered for a long time. They instantly took possession of horses and carriages, and my sister-in-law, toiling up a steep hill, would be passed by her own carriage and horses filled with German officers. However, on the whole, W. said, the Germans, as a victorious invading army, behaved well, the officers always perfectly polite, and keeping their men in good order. They had all sorts and kinds at the château. They rarely remained long—used to appear at the gate in small bands of four or five, with a sous-officier, who always asked to see either the proprietor or someone in authority. He said how many men and horses he wanted lodged and fed, and announced the arrival, a little later, of several officers to dine and sleep. They were always received by M. A. or W., and the same conversation took place every time. They were told the servant would show them their rooms, and their dinner would be served at any hour they wished. They replied that they would have the honour of waiting upon the ladies of the family as soon as they had made a little toilette and removed the dust of the route, and that they would be very happy to dine with the family at their habitual hour. They were then told that the ladies didn't receive, and that the family dined alone. They were always annoyed at that answer. As a rule they behaved well, but occasionally there would be some rough specimens among the officers.

W. was coming home one day from his usual round just before nightfall, when he heard loud voices and a great commotion in the hall—M. A. and one or two German officers. The old man very quiet and dignified, the Germans most insulting, with threats of taking him off to prison. W. interfered at once, and learned from the irate officers what was the cause of the quarrel. They had asked for champagne (with the usual idea of foreigners that champagne flowed through all French châteaux), and M. A. had said there was none in the house. They knew better, as some of their men had seen champagne bottles in the cellar. W. said there was certainly a mistake—there was none in the house. They again became most insolent and threatening—said they would take them both to prison. W. suggested, wouldn't it be better to go down the cellar with him? Then they could see for themselves there was none. Accordingly they all adjourned to the cellar and W. saw at once what had misled them—a quantity of bottles of eau de Seidlitz, rather like champagne bottles in shape. They pointed triumphantly to these and asked what he meant by saying there was no champagne, and told their men to carry off the bottles. W. said again it was not champagne—he didn't believe they would like it. They were quite sure they had found a prize, and all took copious draughts of the water—with disastrous results, as they heard afterward from the servants.

Later, during the armistice and Prussian occupation, there were soldiers quartered all around the château, and, of course, there were many distressing scenes. All our little village of Louvry, near our farm, had taken itself off to the woods. They were quite safe there, as the Prussians never came into the woods on account of the sharpshooters. W. said their camp was comfortable enough—they had all their household utensils, beds, blankets, donkeys, and goats, and could make fires in the clearing in the middle of the woods. They were mostly women and children, only a very few old men and young boys left. The poor things were terrified by the Germans and Bismarck, of whom they had made themselves an extraordinary picture. "Monsieur sait que Bismarck tue tous les enfants pour qu'il n'y ait plus de Français." (Monsieur knows that Bismarck kills all the children so that there shall be no more French.) The boys kept W. in a fever. They had got some old guns, and were always hovering about on the edge of the wood, trying to have a shot at a German. He was very uncomfortable himself at one time during the armistice, for he was sending off parties of recruits to join one of the big corps d'armée in the neighbourhood, and they all passed at the château to get their money and feuille de route, which was signed by him. He sent them off in small bands of four or five, always through the woods, with a line to various keepers and farmers along the route, who could be trusted, and would help them to get on and find their way. Of course, if anyone of them had been taken with W.'s signature and recommendation on him, the Germans would have made short work of W., which he was quite aware of; so every night for weeks his big black Irish horse Paddy was saddled and tied to a certain tree in one of the narrow alleys of the big park—the branches so thick and low that it was difficult to pass in broad daylight, and at night impossible, except for him who knew every inch of the ground. With five minutes' start, if the alarm had been given, he could have got away into his own woods, where he knew no one would follow him.

Hubert, the old coachman, used often to talk to me about all that troubled time. When the weather was dark and stormy he used to stay himself half the night, starting at every sound, and there are so many sounds in the woods at night, all sorts of wild birds and little animals that one never hears in the daytime—sometimes a rabbit would dart out of a hole and whisk round a corner; sometimes a big buse (sort of eagle) would fly out of a tree with great flapping of wings; occasionally a wild-cat with bright-green eyes would come stealthily along and then make a flying leap over the bushes. His nerves were so unstrung that every noise seemed a danger, and he had visions of Germans lying in ambush in the woods, waiting to pounce upon W. if he should appear. He said Paddy was so wise, seemed to know that he must be perfectly quiet, never kicked nor snorted.

It was impossible to realise those dreadful days when we were riding and walking in the woods, so enchanting in the early summer, with thousands of lilies of the valley and periwinkles growing wild, and a beautiful blue flower, a sort of orchid. We used to turn all the village children into the woods, and they picked enormous bunches of lilies, which stood all over the château in china bowls. I loved the wood life at all seasons. I often made the round with W. and his keepers in the autumn when he was preparing a battue. The men were very keen about the game, knew the tracks of all the animals, showing me the long narrow rabbit tracks, running a long distance toward the quarries, which were full of rabbit holes, and the little delicate hoof-marks of the chevreuil (roe-deer) just where he had jumped across the road. The wild boar was easy to trace—little twigs broken, and ferns and leaves quite crushed, where he had passed. The wild boars and stags never stayed very long in our woods—went through merely to the forest of Villers-Cotterets—so it was most important to know the exact moment of their passage, and there was great pride and excitement when one was taken.

Another interesting moment was when the coupe de l'année was being made. Parts of the woods were cut down regularly every year, certain squares marked off. The first day's work was the marking of the big trees along the alleys which were to remain—a broad red ring around the trunks being very conspicuous. Then came the thinning of the trees, cutting off the top branches, and that was really a curious sight. The men climbed high into the tree, and then hung on to the trunk with iron clamps on their feet, with points which stuck into the bark, and apparently gave them a perfectly secure hold, but it looked dangerous to see them swinging off from the trunk with a sort of axe in their hands, cutting off the branches with a swift, sharp stroke. When they finally attacked the big trees that were to come down it was a much longer affair, and they made slow progress. They knew their work well, the exact moment when the last blow had been given, and they must spring aside to get out of the way when the tree fell with a great crash.

There were usually two or three big battues in November for the neighbouring farmers and small proprietors. The breakfast always took place at the keeper's house. We had arranged one room as a dining-room, and the keeper's wife was a very good cook; her omelette au lard and civet de lièvre, classic dishes for a shooting breakfast, were excellent. The repast always ended with a galette aux amandes made by the chef of the château. I generally went down to the kennels at the end of the day, and it was a pretty sight when the party emerged from the woods, first the shooters, then a regiment of beaters (men who track the game), the game cart with a donkey bringing up the rear—the big game, chevreuil or boar, at the bottom of the cart, the hares and rabbits hanging from the sides. The sportsmen all came back to the keeper's lodge to have a drink before starting off on their long drive home, and there was always a great discussion over the entries in the game book and the number of pièces each man had killed. It was a very difficult account to make, as every man counted many more rabbits than the trackers had found, so they were obliged to make an average of the game that had been brought in. When all the guests had departed it was killing to hear the old keeper's criticisms.

There were all sorts and kinds.

Another important function was a large breakfast to all the mayors, conseillers d'arrondissement, and rich farmers of W.'s canton. That always took place at the château, and Mme. A. and I appeared at table. There were all sorts and kinds—some men in dress coats and white gloves, some very rough specimens in corduroys and thick-nailed shoes, having begun life as garçons de ferme (ploughboys). They were all intelligent, well up in politics, and expressed themselves very well, but I think, on the whole, they were pleased when Mme. A. and I withdrew and they went into the gallery for their coffee and cigars. Mme. A. was extraordinarily easy—talked to them all. They came in exactly the same sort of equipage, a light, high, two-wheeled trap with a hood, except the Mayor of La Ferté, our big town, who came in his victoria.

I went often with W. to some of the big farms to see the sheep-shearing and the dairies, and cheese made. The farmer's wife in France is a very capable, hard-working woman—up early, seeing to everything herself, and ruling all her carters and ploughboys with a heavy hand. Once a week, on market day, she takes her cheeses to the market town, driving herself in her high gig, and several times I have seen some of them coming home with a cow tied to their wagon behind, which they had bought at the market. They were always pleased to see us, delighted to show anything we wanted to see, offered us refreshment—bread and cheese, milk and wine—but never came to see me at the château. I made the round of all the châteaux with Mme. A. to make acquaintance with the neighbours. They were all rather far off, but I loved the long drives, almost always through the forest, which was quite beautiful in all seasons, changing like the sea. It was delightful in midsummer, the branches of the big trees almost meeting over our heads, making a perfect shade, and the long, straight, green alleys stretching away before us, as far as we could see. When the wood was a little less thick, the afternoon sun would make long zigzags of light through the trees and trace curious patterns upon the hard white road when we emerged occasionally for a few minutes from the depths of the forest at a cross-road. It was perfectly still, but summer stillness, when one hears the buzzing and fluttering wings of small birds and insects, and is conscious of life around one.

The most beautiful time for the forest is, of course, in the autumn. October and November are lovely months, with the changing foliage, the red and yellow almost as vivid as in America, and always a foreground of moss and brown ferns, which grow very thick and high all through the forest. We used to drive sometimes over a thick carpet of red and yellow leaves, hardly hearing the horses' hoofs or the noise of the wheels, and when we turned our faces homeward toward the sunset there was really a glory of colour in wood and sky. It was always curiously lonely—we rarely met anything or anyone, occasionally a group of wood-cutters or boys exercising dogs and horses from the hunting-stables of Villers-Cotterets. At long intervals we would come to a keeper's lodge, standing quite alone in the middle of the forest, generally near a carrefour where several roads met. There was always a small clearing—garden and kennels, and a perfectly comfortable house, but it must be a lonely life for the women when their husbands are off all day on their rounds. I asked one of them once, a pretty, smiling young woman who always came out when the carriage passed, with three or four children hanging to her skirts, if she was never afraid, being alone with small children and no possibility of help, if any drunkards or evilly disposed men came along. She said no—that tramps and vagabonds never came into the heart of the forest, and always kept clear of the keeper's house, as they never knew where he and his gun might be. She said she had had one awful night with a sick child. She was alone in the house with two other small children, almost babies, while her husband had to walk several miles to get a doctor. The long wait was terrible. I got to know all the keepers' wives on our side of the forest quite well, and it was always a great interest to them when we passed on horseback, so few women rode in that part of France in those days.

Sometimes, when we were in the heart of the forest, a stag with wide-spreading antlers would bound across the road; sometimes a pretty roebuck would come to the edge of the wood and gallop quickly back as we got near.

We had a nice couple at the lodge, an old cavalry soldier who had been for years coachman at the château and who had married a Scotchwoman, nurse of one of the children. It was curious to see the tall, gaunt figure of the Scotchwoman, always dressed in a short linsey skirt, loose jacket, and white cap, in the midst of the chattering, excitable women of the village. She looked so unlike them. Our peasant women wear, too, a short thick skirt, loose jacket, and worsted or knit stockings, but they all wear sabots and on their heads a turban made of bright-coloured cotton; the older women, of course—the girls wear nothing on their heads. They become bent and wrinkled very soon—old women before their time—having worked always in the fields and carried heavy burdens on their backs. The Scotchwoman kept much to herself and rarely left the park. But all the women came to her with their troubles. Nearly always the same story—the men spending their earnings on drink and the poor mothers toiling and striving from dawn till dark to give the little ones enough to eat. She was a strict Protestant, very taciturn and reserved, quite the type of the old Calvinist race who fought so hard against the "Scarlet Woman" when the beautiful and unhappy Mary Stuart was reigning in Scotland and trying to rule her wild subjects. I often went to see her and she would tell me of her first days at the château, where everything was so different from what she was accustomed to.

She didn't tell me what Mme. A. did—that she was a very handsome girl and all the men of the establishment fell in love with her. There were dramas of jealousy when she finally decided to marry the coachman. Our chef had learned how to make various English cakes in London, and whenever he made buns or a plum-pudding we used to take some to her. She was a great reader, and we always kept the *Times* for her, and she and I sympathised with each other—two Anglo-Saxons married in France.

Some of the traditions of the château were quite charming. I was sitting in the lodge one day talking to Mme. Antoine, when the baker appeared with what seemed to me an extraordinary provision of bread. I said, "Does he leave the bread for the whole village with you?" "It is not for me, madame, it is for the traînards (tramps) who pass on the road," and she explained that all the châteaux gave a piece of bread and two sous to any wayfarer who asked for food. She cut the bread into good thick slices, and showed me a wooden bowl on the chimney, filled with two-sous pieces. While I was there two men appeared at the big gates, which were always open in the day. They were strong young fellows carrying their bundles, and a sort of pitchfork slung over their shoulders. They looked weary and foot-sore, their shoes worn in holes. They asked for something to drink and some tobacco, didn't care very much for the water, which was all that Mme. Antoine had to give them, but thanked her civilly enough for the bread and sous.

The park wall was a good vantage-ground to see all (and that wasn't much) that went on on the highroad. The diligence to Meaux passed twice a day, with a fine rattle of old wheels and chains, and cracking of whips. It went down the steep hill well enough, but coming up was quite another affair. All the passengers and the driver got out always, and even then it was difficult to get the heavy, cumbersome vehicle up the hill, in winter particularly, when the roads were muddy and slippery. The driver knew us all well, and was much interested in all that went on at the château. He often brought parcels, and occasionally people from the village who wanted to see W.—sometimes a blind piano-tuner who came from Villers-Cotterets. He was very kind to the poor blind man, helped him down most carefully from the diligence, and always brought him through the park gates to the lodge, where he delivered him over to Antoine. It was curious to see the blind man at work. Once he had been led through the rooms, he was quite at home, found the pianos, fussed over the keys and the strings, exactly as if he saw everything. He tuned all the pianos in the country, and was much pleased to put his hands on one that wasn't fifty years old. I had brought down my new Erard.

Sometimes a country wedding passed, and that was always a pretty sight. A marriage is always an important affair in France in every class of life. There are long discussions with all the members of the two families. The curé, the notary, the patron (if the young man is a workman), are all consulted, and there are as many negotiations and agreements in the most humble families as in the grand monde of the Faubourg St. Germain. Almost all French parents give a dot of some kind to their children, and whatever the sum is, either five hundred francs or two thousand, it is always scrupulously paid over to the notary. The wedding-day is a long one. After the religious ceremony in the church, all the wedding party—members of the two families and a certain number of friends—adjourn to the hotel of the little town for a breakfast, which is long and most abundant. Then comes the crowning glory of the day—a country walk along the dusty highroad to some wood or meadow where they can spend the whole afternoon. It is pretty to see the little procession trudging along—the bride in all her wedding garments, white dress, white shoes, wreath, and veil; the groom in a dress coat, top-hat, white cravat and waistcoat, with a white ribbon bow on his sleeve. Almost all the girls and young women are dressed in white or light colours; the mothers and grandmothers (the whole family turns out) in black with flowers in their bonnets. There is usually a fiddler walking ahead making most remarkable sounds on his old cracked instrument, and the younger members of the party take an occasional gallop along the road. They are generally very gay; there is much laughing, and from time to time a burst of song. It is always a mystery to me how the bride keeps her dress and petticoat so clean, but she does, with that extraordinary knack all Frenchwomen seem to have of holding up their skirts. They passed often under the wall of the château, for a favourite resting-place was in our woods at the entrance of the allée verte, where it widens out a little; the moss makes a beautiful soft carpet, and the big trees give perfect shade. We heard sounds of merriment one day when we were passing and we stopped to look on, from behind the bushes, where we couldn't be seen. There was quite a party assembled. The fiddler was playing some sort of country-dance and all the company, except the very old people, were dancing and singing, some of the men indulging in most wonderful steps and capers. The children were playing and running under the trees. One stout man was asleep, stretched out full length on the side of the road. I fancy his piquette, as they call the ordinary white wine of the country, had been too much for him. The bride and groom were strolling about a little apart from the others, quite happy and lover-like, his arm around her waist, she blushing and giggling.

The gendarmes passed also very regularly. They always stopped and talked, had a drink with Antoine, and gave all the local news—how many braconniers (poachers) had been caught, how long they were to stay in prison, how some of the farmers' sheep had disappeared, no one knew how exactly—there were no more robbers. One day two of them passed, dragging a man between them who had evidently been struggling and fighting. His blouse was torn, and there was a great gash on his face. We were wildly excited, of course. They told us he was an old sinner, a poacher who had been in prison various times, but these last days, not contented with setting traps for the rabbits, he had set fire to some of the hay-stacks, and they had been hunting for him for some time. He looked a rough customer, had an ugly scowl on his face. One of the little hamlets near the château, on the canal, was a perfect nest of poachers, and I had continual struggles with the keepers when I gave clothes or blankets to the women and children. They said some of the women were as bad as the men, and that I ought not to encourage them to come up to the house and beg for food and clothing; that they sold all the little jackets and petticoats we gave them to the canal hands (also a bad lot) for brandy. I believe it was true in some cases, but in the middle of winter, with snow on the ground (we were hardly warm in the house with big fires everywhere), I couldn't send away women with four or five children, all insufficiently clothed and fed, most of them in cotton frocks with an old worn knit shawl around their shoulders, legs and arms bare and chapped, half frozen. Some of them lived in caverns or great holes in the rocks, really like beasts. On the road to La Ferté there was a big hole (there is no other word for it) in the bank where a whole family lived. The man was always in prison for something, and his wife, a tall, gaunt figure, with wild hair and eyes, spent most of her time in the woods teaching her boys to set traps for the game. The curé told us that one of the children was ill, and that there was literally nothing in the house, so I took one of my cousins with me, and we climbed up the bank, leaving the carriage with Hubert, the coachman, expostulating seriously below. We came to a rickety old door which practically consisted of two rotten planks nailed together. It was ajar; clouds of black smoke poured out as we opened it, and it was some time before we could see anything. We finally made out a heap of filthy rags in one corner near a sort of fire made of charred pieces of black peat. Two children, one a boy about twelve years old, was lying on the heap of rags, coughing his heart out. He hardly raised his head when we came in. Another child, a girl, some two years younger, was lying beside him, both of them frightfully thin and white; one saw nothing but great dark eyes in their faces. The mother was crouched on the floor close to the children. She hardly moved at first, and was really a terrifying object when she got up; half savage, scarcely clothed—a short petticoat in holes and a ragged bodice gaping open over her bare skin, no shoes or stockings; big black eyes set deep in her head, and a quantity of unkempt black hair. She looked enormous when she stood up, her head nearly touching the roof. I didn't feel very comfortable, but we were two, and the carriage and Hubert within call. The woman was civil enough when she saw I had not come empty-handed. We took her some soup, bread, and milk. The children pounced upon the bread like little wild animals. The mother didn't touch anything while we were there—said she was glad to have the milk for the boy. I never saw human beings living in such utter filth and poverty. A crofter's cottage in Scotland, or an Irish hovel with the pigs and children all living together, was a palace compared to that awful hole. I remonstrated vigorously with W. and the Mayor of La Ferté for allowing people to live in that way, like beasts, upon the highroad, close to a perfectly prosperous country town. However, they were vagrants, couldn't live anywhere, for when we passed again, some days later, there was no one in the hole. The door had fallen down, there was no smoke coming out, and the neighbours told us the family had suddenly disappeared. The authorities then took up the matter—the holes were filled up, and no one was allowed to live in them. It really was too awful—like the dwellers in caves of primeval days.

We didn't have many visits at the château, though we were so near Paris (only about an hour and a half by the express), but the old people had got accustomed to their quiet life, and visitors would have worried them. Sometimes a Protestant pasteur would come down for two days. We had a nice visit once from M. de Pressensé, father of the present deputy, one of the most charming, cultivated men one could imagine. He talked easily and naturally, using beautiful language. He was most interesting when he told us about the Commune, and all the horrors of that time in Paris. He was in the Tuileries when the mob sacked and burned the palace; saw the femmes de la halle sitting on the brocade and satin sofas, saying, "C'est nous les princesses maintenant"; saw the entrance of the troops from Versailles, and the quantity of innocent people shot who were merely standing looking on at the barricades, having never had a gun in their hands. The only thing I didn't like was his long extempore (to me familiar) prayers at night. I believe it is a habit in some old-fashioned French Protestant families to pray for each member of the family by name. I thought it was bad enough when he prayed for the new ménage just beginning their married life (that was us), that they might be spiritually guided to do their best for each other and their respective families; but when he proceeded to *name* some others of the family who had strayed a little from the straight and narrow path, hoping they would be brought to see, by Divine grace, the error of their ways, I was horrified, and could hardly refrain from expressing my opinion to the old people. However, I was learning prudence, and when my opinion and judgment were diametrically opposed to those of my new family (which happened often) I kept them to myself. Sunday was strictly kept. There was no Protestant church anywhere near. We had a service in the morning in M. A.'s library. He read prayers and a short sermon, all the household appearing, as most of the servants were Swiss and Protestants. In the afternoon Mme. A. had all the village children at the château. She had a small organ in one of the rooms in the wing of the dining-room, taught them hymns and read them simple little stories. The curé was rather anxious at first, having his little flock under such a dangerous heretic influence, but he very soon realized what an excellent thing it was for the children, and both he and the mothers were much disappointed when anything happened to put off the lesson. They didn't see much of the curé. He would pay one formal visit in the course of the year, but there was never any intimacy.

We lived much for ourselves, and for a few months in the year it was a rest and change from Paris, and the busy, agitated life, social and political, that one always led there. I liked the space, too, the great high, empty rooms, with no frivolous little tables and screens or stuff on the walls, no photograph stands nor fancy vases for flowers, no bibelot of any kind—large, heavy pieces of furniture which were always found every morning in exactly the same place. Once or twice, in later years, I tried to make a few changes, but it was absolutely useless to contend with a wonderful old servant called Ferdinand, who was over sixty years old, and had been brought up at the château, had always remained there with the various owners, and who knew every nook and corner of the house and everything that was in it. It was years before I succeeded in talking to him. I used to meet him sometimes on the stairs and corridors, always running, and carrying two or three pails and brooms. If he could, he dived into any open door when he saw me coming, and apparently never heard me when I spoke, for he never answered. He was a marvellous servant, cleaned the whole house, opened and shut all the windows night and morning (almost work enough for one man), lit the calorifères, scrubbed and swept and polished floors from early dawn until ten o'clock, when we left the salon. He never lived with the other servants, cooked his own food at his own hours in his room, and his only companion was a large black cat, which always followed him about. He did W.'s service, and W. said that they used to talk about all sorts of things, but I fancy master and servant were equally reticent and understood each other without many words.

I slipped one day on the very slippery wooden steps leading from W.'s little study to the passage. Baby did the same, and got a nasty fall on the stone flags, so I asked W. if he would ask Ferdinand to put a strip of carpet on the steps (there were only four). W. gave the order, but no carpet appeared. He repeated it rather curtly. The old Ferdinand made no answer, but grumbled to himself over his broom that it was perfectly foolish and useless to put down a piece of carpet, that for sixty years people and children, and babies, had walked down those steps and no one had ever thought of asking for carpets. W. had really rather to apologize and explain that his wife was nervous and unused to such highly polished floors. However, we became great friends afterward, Ferdinand and I, and when he understood how fond I was of the château, he didn't mind my deranging the furniture a little. Two grand pianos were a great trial to him. I think he would have liked to put one on top of the other.

The library, quite at one end of the house, separated from the drawing-room we always sat in by a second large salon, was a delightful, quiet resort when any one wanted to read or write. There were quantities of books, French, English, and German—the classics in all three languages, and a fine collection of historical memoirs.

Ferdinand.

II

COUNTRY VISITS

We didn't pay many visits; but sometimes, when the weather was fine and there was no hunting, and W. gone upon an expedition to some outlying village, Mme. A. and I would start off for one of the neighbouring châteaux. We went one day to the château de C., where there was a large family party assembled, four generations—the old grandmother, her son and daughter, both married, the daughter's daughter, also married, and her children. It was a pretty drive, about an hour all through the forest. The house is quite modern, not at all pretty, a square white building, with very few trees near it, the lawn and one or two flower-beds not particularly well kept. The grounds ran straight down to the Villers-Cotterets forest, where M. M. has good shooting. The gates were open, the concierge said the ladies were there. (They didn't have to be summoned by a bell. That is one of the habits of this part of the country. There is almost always a large bell at the stable or "communs," and when visitors arrive and the family are out in the grounds, not too far off, they are summoned by the bell. I was quite surprised one day at Bourneville, when we were in the woods at some little distance from the château, when we heard the bell, and my companion, a niece of Mme. A., instantly turned back, saying, "That means there are visits; we must go back.") We found all the ladies sitting working in a corner salon with big windows opening on the park. The old grandmother was knitting, but she was so straight and slight, with bright black eyes, that it wouldn't have seemed at all strange to see her bending over an embroidery frame like all the others. The other three ladies were each seated at an embroidery frame in the embrasures of the windows. I was much impressed, particularly with the large pieces of work that they were undertaking, a portière, covers for the billiard-table, bed, etc. It quite recalled what one had always read of feudal France, when the seigneur would be off with his retainers hunting or fighting, and the châtelaine, left alone in the château, spent her time in her "bower" surrounded by her maidens, all working at the wonderful tapestries one sees still in some of the old churches and convents. I was never much given to work, but I made a mental resolve that I, too, would set up a frame in one of the drawing-rooms at home, and had visions of yards of pale-blue satin, all covered with wonderful flowers and animals, unrolling themselves under my skilful fingers—but I must confess that it remained a vision. I never got further than little crochet petticoats, which clothed every child in the village. To make the picture complete there should have been a page in velvet cap and doublet, stretched on the floor at the feet of his mistress, trying to distract her with songs and ballads. The master of the house, M. M., was there, having come in from shooting. He had been reading aloud to the ladies—Alfred de Musset, I think. That part of the picture I could never realize, as there is nothing W. loathes like reading aloud except, perhaps, being read to.

"Merci, je vais bien."

Long pauses when nobody seemed to have anything to say.

They were very friendly and easy, showed us the downstairs part of the house, and gave us goûter, not tea, wine and cake. The house looked comfortable enough, nothing picturesque; a large square hall with horns, whips, foxes' brushes, antlers, and all sorts of trophies of the chase on the walls. They are sporting people; all ride. The dining-room, a large bright room, was panelled with life-size portraits of the family: M. and Mme. M. in hunting dress, green coats, tricorne hats, *on* their horses; the daughter of the house and one of her brothers, rowing in a boat on a small lake; the eldest son in shooting dress, corduroys, his gun slung over his shoulder, his dog by his side. They were all very like.

We strolled about the garden a little, and saw lots of pheasants walking peacefully about at the edge of the woods. They made me promise to come back one day with W., he to shoot and I to walk about with the ladies. We saw the children of the fourth generation, and left with the impression of a happy, simple family party. M. M. was a conseiller général of the Aisne and a colleague of W.'s. They always stayed at the same hotel (de la Hure) in Laon at the time of the conseil général, and M. M. was much amused at first with W.'s baggage: a large bath-tub, towels (for in small French provincial hotels towels were microscopic and few in number), and a package of tea, which was almost an unknown commodity in those days. None of our visitors ever took any, and always excused themselves with the same phrase, "Merci, je vais bien," evidently looking upon it as some strange and hurtful medicine. That has all changed, like everything else. Now one finds tea not only at all the châteaux, with brioches and toast, but even in all the hotels, but I wouldn't guarantee what we get there as ever having seen China or Ceylon, and it is still wiser to take chocolate or coffee, which is almost always good. We had a lovely drive back. The forest was beautiful in the waning light. As usual, we didn't meet any vehicle of any kind, and were quite excited when we saw a carriage approaching in the distance—however, it proved to be W. in his dog-cart. We passed through one or two little villages quite lost in the forest—always the same thing, one long, straggling street, with nobody in it, a large farm at one end and very often the church at the other. As it was late, the farm gates were all open, the cattle inside, teams of white oxen drinking out of a large trough.

In a large farm near Boursonne there was much animation and conversation. All the beasts were in, oxen, cows, horses, chickens, and in one corner, a flock of geese. The poor little "goose girl," a child about ten years old with bright-blue eyes and a pig-tail like straw hanging down her back, was being scolded violently by the farmer's wife, who was presiding in person over the rentrée of the animals, for having brought her geese home on a run. They wouldn't eat, and would certainly all be ill, and probably die before morning. There is a pretty little old château at Boursonne; the park, however, so shut in by high walls that one sees nothing in passing. W. had shot there once or twice in former years, but it has changed hands very often.

Sometimes we paid more humble visits, not to châteaux, but to the principal people of the little country town near, from which we had all our provisions. We went to see the doctor's wife, the notary's wife, the mayor's wife, and the two schools—the asile or infant school, and the more important school for bigger girls.

The old doctor was quite a character, had been for years in the country, knew everybody and everybody's private history. He was the doctor of the château, by the year, attended to everybody, masters and servants, and received a regular salary, like a secretary. He didn't come very often for us in his medical capacity, but he often dropped in at the end of the day to have a talk with W. The first time I saw him W. presented him to me, as un bon ami de la famille. I naturally put out my hand, which so astonished and disconcerted him (he barely touched the tips of my fingers) that I was rather bewildered. W. explained after he had gone that in that class of life in France they never shook hands with a lady, and that the poor man was very much embarrassed. He was very useful to W. as a political agent, as he was kind to the poor people and took small (or no) fees. They all loved him, and talked to him quite freely. His women-kind were very shy and provincial. I think our visits were a great trial to them. They always returned them most punctiliously, and came in all their best clothes. When we went to see them we generally found them in short black skirts, and when they were no longer very young, with black caps, but they always had handsome silk dresses, velvet cloaks, and hats with flowers and feathers when they came to see us. Some of them took the cup of tea we offered, but they didn't know what to do with it, and sat on the edge of their chairs, looking quite miserable until we relieved them of the burden of the tea-cup. Mme. A. was rather against the tea-table; she preferred the old-fashioned tray handed around with wine and cakes, but I persuaded her to try, and after a little while she acknowledged that it was better to have the tea-table brought in. It made a diversion; I got up to make the tea. Someone gave me a chair, someone else handed the cups. It made a little movement, and was not so stiff as when we all sat for over an hour on the same chairs making conversation. It is terrible to have to make conversation, and extraordinary how little one finds to say. We had always talked easily enough at home, but then things came more naturally, and even the violent family discussions were amusing, but my recollection of these French provincial visits is something awful. Everybody so polite, so stiff, and the long pauses when nobody seemed to have anything to say. I of course was a novelty and a foreign element—they didn't quite know what to do with me. Even to Mme. A., and I grew very fond of her, and she was invariably charming to me, I was something different. We had many talks on every possible subject during our long drives, and also in the winter afternoons. At first I had my tea always upstairs in my own little salon, which I loved with the curtains drawn, a bright wood-fire burning, and all my books about; but when I found that she sat alone in the big drawing-room, not able to occupy herself in any way, I asked her if I might order my tea there, and there were very few afternoons that I didn't sit with her when I was at home. She talked often about her early married life—winters in Cannes and in Paris, where they received a great deal, principally Protestants, and I fancy she sometimes regretted the interchange of ideas and the brilliant conversation she had been accustomed to, but she never said it. She was never tired of hearing about my early days in America—our family life—the extraordinary liberty of the young people, etc. We often talked over the religious question, and though we were both Protestants, we were as far apart almost as if one was a pagan. Protestantism in France always has seemed to me such a rigid form of worship, so little calculated to influence young people or draw them to church. The plain, bare churches with white-washed walls, the long sermons and extempore prayers, speaking so much of the anger of God and the terrible punishments awaiting the sinner, the trials and sorrows that must come to all. I often think of a sermon I heard preached in one Protestant church, to the boys and girls who were making their first communion—all little things, the girls in their white frocks and long white veils, the boys with white waistcoats and white ribbons on their arms, making such a pretty group as they sat on the front benches listening hard to all the preacher said. I wondered that the young, earnest faces didn't suggest something to him besides the horrors of eternal punishment, the wickedness and temptations of the world they were going to face, but his only idea seemed to be that he must warn them of all the snares and temptations that were going to beset their paths. Mme. A. couldn't understand my ideas when I said I loved the Episcopal service—the prayers and litany I had always heard, the Easter and Christmas hymns I had always sung, the carols, the anthems, the great organ, the flowers at Easter, the greens at Christmas. All that seemed to her to be a false sentiment appealing to the senses and imagination. "But if it brings people to church, and the beautiful music elevates them and raises their thoughts to higher things—" "That is not religion; real religion means the prayer of St. Chrysostom, 'Where two or three are gathered together in My name I will grant their requests.'" "That is very well for really religious, strong people who think out their religion and don't care for any outward expression of it, but for weaker souls who want to be helped, and who are helped by the beautiful music and the familiar prayers, surely it is better to give them something that brings them to church and makes them better men and women than to frighten them away with such strict, uncompromising doctrines—" "No, that is only sentiment, not real religious feeling." I don't think we ever understood each other any better on that subject, and we discussed it so often.

Mme. A., with whom I made my round of calls at the neighbouring châteaux, was a charming companion. She had lived a great deal in Paris, in the Protestant coterie, which was very intellectual and cultivated. The salons of the Duchesse de Broglie, Mmes. de Staël, d'Haussonville, Guizot, were most interesting and recherchés, very exclusive and very serious, but a centre for all political and literary talk. I have often heard my husband say some of the best talkers in society s'étaient formés dans ces salons, where, as young men, they listened modestly to all the brilliant conversation going on around them.

It was an exception when we found anyone at home when we called in the neighbourhood, and when we did, it was evident that afternoon visits were a rarity. We did get in one cold November afternoon, and our visit was a sample of many others that we paid.

The door was opened by a footman struggling into his coat, with a handful of faggots in his arms. He ushered us through several bare, stiff, cold rooms (proportions handsome enough) to a smaller salon, which the family usually occupied. Then he lighted a fire (which consisted principally of smoke) and went to summon his mistress. The living-room was just as bare and stiff as the others, no trace of anything that looked like habitation or what we should consider comfort—no books nor work nor flowers (that, however, is comparatively recent in France). I remember quite well Mme. Casimir-Périer telling me that when she went with her husband to St. Petersburg about fifty years ago, one of the things that struck her most in the Russian salons, was the quantity of green plants and cut flowers—she had never seen them in France. There were often fine pictures, tapestries, and furniture, all the chairs in a row against the wall.

Then he lighted a fire.

Our visits were always long, as most of the châteaux were at a certain distance, and we were obliged to stay an hour and a half, sometimes longer, to rest the horses. It was before the days of five-o'clock tea. A tray was brought in with sweet wine (Malaga or Vin de Chypre) and cakes (ladies'-fingers) which evidently had figured often before on similar occasions. Conversation languished sometimes, though Mme. A. was wonderful, talking so easily about everything. In the smaller places, when people rarely went to Paris, it ran always in the same grooves—the woods, the hunting (very good in the Villers-Cotterets forest), the schoolmaster (so difficult to get proper books for the children to read), the curé, and all local gossip, and as much about the iniquities of the republic as could be said before the wife of a republican senator. Wherever we went, even to the largest châteaux, where the family went to Paris for the season, the talk was almost entirely confined to France and French interests. Books, politics, music, people, nothing existed apparently au-delà des frontières. America was an unknown quantity. It was strange to see intelligent people living in the world so curiously indifferent as to what went on in other countries. At first I used to talk a little about America and Rome, where I had lived many years and at such an interesting time—the last days of Pio Nono and the transformation of the old superstitious papal Rome to the capital of young Italy—but I soon realized that it didn't interest any one, and by degrees I learned to talk like all the rest.

I often think of one visit to a charming little Louis XV château standing quite on the edge of the forest—just room enough for the house, and the little hamlet at the gates; a magnificent view of the forest, quite close to the lawn behind the château, and then sweeping off, a dark-blue mass, as far as one could see. We were shown into a large, high room, no carpet, no fire, some fine portraits, very little furniture, all close against the wall, a round table in the middle with something on it, I couldn't make out what at first. Neither books, reviews, nor even a photographic album—the supreme resource of provincial salons. When we got up to take leave I managed to get near the table, and the *ornament* was a large white plate with a piece of fly-paper on it. The mistress of the house was shy and uncomfortable; sent at once for her husband, and withdrew from the conversation as soon as he appeared, leaving him to make all the "frais." We walked a little around the park before leaving. It was really a lovely little place, with its background of forest and the quiet, sleepy little village in front; very lonely and far from everything, but with a certain charm of its own. Two or three dogs were playing in the court-yard, and one curious little animal who made a rush at the strangers. I was rather taken aback, particularly when the master of the house told me not to be afraid, it was only a marcassin (small wild boar), who had been born on the place, and was as quiet as a kitten. I did not think the great tusks and square, shaggy head looked very pleasant, but the little thing was quiet enough, came and rubbed itself against its master's legs and played quite happily with the dogs. We heard afterward that they were obliged to kill it. It grew fierce and unmanageable, and no one would come near the place.

I took Henrietta with me sometimes when I had a distant visit to pay; an hour and a half's drive alone on a country road where you never meet anything was rather dull. We went one cold December afternoon to call upon Mme. B., the widow of an old friend and colleague of W.'s. We were in the open carriage, well wrapped up, and enjoyed the drive immensely. The country looked beautiful in the bright winter sunshine, the distant forest always in a blue mist, the trees with their branches white with "givre" (hoarfrost), and patches of snow and ice all over the fields.

For a wonder we didn't go through the forest—drove straight away from it and had charming effects of colour upon some of the thatched cottages in the villages we passed through; one or two had been mended recently and the mixture of old brown, bright red and glistening white was quite lovely.

We went almost entirely along the great plains, occasionally small bits of wood and very fair hills as we got near our destination. The villages always very scattered and almost deserted—when it is cold everybody stays indoors—and of course there is no work to be done on the farms when the ground is hard frozen. It is a difficult question to know what to do with the men of all the small hamlets when the real winter sets in; the big farms turn off many of their labourers, and as it is a purely agricultural country all around us there is literally nothing to do. My husband and several of the owners of large estates gave work to many with their regular "coupe" of wood, but that only lasts a short time, and the men who are willing to work but can find nothing drift naturally into cafés and billiard saloons, where they read cheap bad papers and talk politics of the wildest description.

We found our château very well situated on the top of a hill, a good avenue leading up to the gate, a pretty little park with fine trees at the back, the tower of the village church just visible through the trees at the end of the central alley. It was hardly a château—half manor, half farm. We drove into a large courtyard, or rather farmyard, quite deserted; no one visible anywhere; the door of the house was open, but there was no bell nor apparently any means of communicating with any one. Hubert cracked his whip noisily several times without any result—and we were just wondering what we should do (perhaps put our cards under a stone on the steps) when a man appeared, said Mme. B. was at home, but she was in the stable looking after a sick cow—he would go and tell her we were there. In a few minutes she appeared attired in a short, rusty-black skirt, sabots on her feet, and a black woollen shawl over her head and shoulders. She seemed quite pleased to see us—was not at all put out at being caught in such very simple attire—begged us to come in and ushered us through a long, narrow hall and several cold, comfortless rooms, the shutters not open and no fire anywhere, into her bedroom. All the furniture—chairs, tables and bed—was covered with linen. She explained that it was her "lessive" (general wash) she had just made, that all the linen was *dry*, but she had not had time to put it away. She called a maid and they cleared off two chairs—she sat on the bed.

It was frightfully cold—we were thankful we had kept our wraps on. She said she supposed we would like a fire after our long, cold drive, and rang for a man to bring some wood. He (in his shirt sleeves) appeared with two or three logs of wood and was preparing to make a fire with them all, but she stopped him, said one log was enough, the ladies were not going to stay long—so, naturally, we had no fire and clouds of smoke. She was very talkative, never stopped—told us all about her servants, her husband's political campaigns and how W. would never have been named to the Conseil Général if M.B. hadn't done all his work for him. She asked a great many questions, answering them all herself; then said, "I don't offer you any tea, as I know you always go back to have your tea at home, and I am quite sure you don't want any wine."

There was such an evident reluctance to give us anything that I didn't like to insist, and said we must really be going as we had a long drive before us, though I should have liked something hot; tea, of course, she knew nothing about, but even a glass of ordinary hot wine, which they make very well in France, would have been acceptable. Henrietta was furious; she was shivering with cold, her eyes smarting with the smoke, and not at all interested in M.B.'s political career, or Madame's servants, and said she would have been thankful to have even a glass of vin de Chypre.

It was unfortunate, perhaps, that we had arrived during the "lessive"; that is always a most important function in France. In almost all the big houses in the country (small ones, too) that is the way they do their washing; once a month or once every three months, according to the size of the establishment, the whole washing of the household is done; all the linen: master's, servants', guests'; house is turned out; the linen closets cleaned and aired! Every one looks busy and energetic. It is quite a long affair—lasts three or four days. I often went to see the performance when we made our "lessive" at the château every month.

It always interested our English and American friends, as the washing is never done in that way in either of their countries. It was very convenient at our place as we had plenty of room. The "lavoir" stood at the top of the steps leading into the kitchen gardens; there was a large, square tank sunk in the ground, so that the women could kneel to their work, then a little higher another of beautiful clear water, all under cover. Just across the path there was a small house with a blazing wood fire; in the middle an enormous tub where all the linen was passed through wood ashes. There were four "lessiveuses" (washerwomen), sturdy peasant women with very short skirts, sabots, and turbans (made of blue and white checked calico) on their heads, their strong red arms bared above the elbow. The Mère Michon, the eldest of the four, directed everything and kept them well at work, allowed very little talking; they generally chatter when they are washing and very often quarrel. When they are washing at the public "lavoir" in the village one hears their shrill voices from a great distance. Our "lingère," Mme. Hubert, superintended the whole operation; she was very keen about it and remonstrated vigorously when they slapped the linen too hard sometimes with the little flat sticks, like spades, they use. The linen all came out beautifully white and smooth, hadn't the yellow look that all city-washed clothes have.

I think Mme. B. was very glad to get rid of us, and to begin folding her linen and putting it back in the big wooden wardrobes, that one sees everywhere in France. Some of the old Norman wardrobes, with handsome brass locks and beautifully carved doors, are real works of art—very difficult to get and very expensive.

Fifty years ago the peasant did not understand the value of such a "meuble" and parted with it easily—but now, with railways everywhere and strangers and bric-à-brac people always on the lookout for a really old piece of furniture, they understand quite well that they possess a treasure and exact its full value.

Our drive back was rather shorter, downhill almost all the way, the horses going along at a good steady trot, knowing they were going home.

When we drew up at our own door Hubert remarked respectfully that he thought it was the first time that Madame and Mademoiselle had ever been received by a lady in sabots.

We wondered afterward if she had personally attended to the cow—in the way of poulticing or rubbing it. She certainly didn't wash her hands afterward, and it rather reminded me of one of Charles de Bunsen's stories when he was Secretary of Legation at Turin. In the summer they took a villa in the country just out of the town and had frequent visitors to lunch or dinner. One day two of their friends, Italians, had spent the whole day with them; had walked in the garden, picked fruit and flowers, played with the child and the dogs and the pony, and as they were coming back to the house for dinner, Charles suggested that they might like to come up to his dressing-room and wash their hands before dinner—to which one of them replied, "Grazie, non mi sporco facilmente" (literal translation, "Thanks, I don't dirty myself easily"), and declined the offer of soap and water.

We paid two or three visits one year to the neighbouring châteaux, and had one very pleasant afternoon at the Château de Pinon, belonging to the Courval family. W. had known the late proprietor, the Vicomte de Courval, very well. They had been colleagues of the Conseil Général of the Aisne, were both very fond of the country and country life, and used to have long talks in the evening, when the work of the day was over, about plantation, cutting down trees, preservation of game, etc. Without these talks, I think W. would have found the evenings at the primitive little Hôtel de la Hure, at Laon, rather tedious.

The château is not very old and has no historic interest. It was built by a Monsieur du Bois, Vicomte de Courval, at the end of the seventeenth century. He lived at first in the old feudal château of which nothing now remains. Already times were changing—the thick walls, massive towers, high, narrow windows, almost slits, and deep moat, which were necessary in the old troubled days, when all isolated châteaux might be called upon, at any time, to defend themselves from sudden attack, had given way to the larger and more spacious residences of which Mansard, the famous architect of Louis XIV, has left so many chefs d'oeuvre. It was to Mansard that M. de Courval confided the task of building the château as it now stands, while the no less famous Le Notre was charged to lay out the park and gardens.

It was an easy journey from B— —ville to Pinon. An hour's drive through our beautiful forest of Villers-Cotterets and another hour in the train. We stopped at the little station of Anizy just outside the gates of the park; a brougham was waiting for us and a very short drive through a stately avenue brought us to the drawbridge and the iron gates of the "Cour d'honneur." The house looked imposing; I had an impression of a very high and very long façade with two towers stretching out into the court-yard, which is very large, with fine old trees and broad parterres of bright-coloured flowers on either side of the steps. There was a wide moat of running water, the banks covered with shrubs and flowers—the flowers were principally salvias and chrysanthemums, as it was late in the season, but they made a warm bit of colour. The house stands low, as do all houses surrounded by a moat, but the park rises a little directly behind it and there is a fine background of wood.

We drew up at a flight of broad, shallow steps; the doors were open. There were three or four footmen in the ante-room. While we were taking off our wraps Mme. de Courval appeared; she was short, stout, dressed in black, with that terrible black cap which all widows wear in France—so different from the white cap and soft white muslin collar and cuffs we are accustomed to. She had a charming, easy manner and looked very intelligent and capable. It seems she managed the property extremely well, made the tour of the house, woods and garden every day with her "régisseur." W. had the highest opinion of her business capacity—said she knew the exact market value of everything on the place—from an old tree that must be cut down for timber to the cheeses the farmer's wife made and sold at the Soissons market.

She suggested that I should come upstairs to leave my heavy coat. We went up a broad stone staircase, the walls covered with pictures and engravings; one beautiful portrait of her daughter, the Marquise de Chaponay, on horseback. There were handsome carved chests and china vases on the landing, which opened on a splendid long gallery, very high and light—bedrooms on one side, on the other big windows (ten or twelve, I should think) looking over the park and gardens. She took me to a large, comfortable room, bright wood fire blazing, and a pretty little dressing-room opening out of it, furnished in a gay, old-fashioned pattern of chintz. She said breakfast would be ready in ten minutes—supposed I could find my way down, and left me to my own devices.

I found the family assembled in the drawing-room; four women: Mme. de Courval and her daughter, the Marquise de Chaponay, a tall handsome woman, and two other ladies of a certain age; I did not catch their names, but they looked like all the old ladies one always sees in a country house in France. I should think they were cousins or habituées of the château, as they each had their embroidery frame and one a little dog. I am haunted by the embroidery frames—I am sure I shall end my days in a black cap, bending over a frame making portières or a piano-cover.

We breakfasted in a large square dining-room running straight through the house, windows on each side. The room was all in wood panelling—light gray—the sun streaming in through the windows. Mme. de Courval put W. on her right, me on her other side. We had an excellent breakfast, which we appreciated after our early start. There was handsome old silver on the table and sideboard, which is a rare thing in France, as almost all the silver was melted during the Revolution. Both Mme. de Courval and her daughter were very easy and animated. The Marquise de Chaponay told me she had known W. for years, that in the old days before he became such a busy man and so engrossed in politics he used to read Alfred de Musset to her, in her atelier, while she painted. She supposed he read now to me—which he certainly never did—as he always told me he hated reading aloud. They talked politics, of course, but their opinions were the classic Faubourg St. Germain opinions: "A Republic totally unfitted for France and the French"—"none of the gentlemen in France really Republican at heart" (with evidently a few exceptions)—W.'s English blood and education having, of course, influenced him.

As soon as breakfast was over one of the windows on the side of the moat was opened and we all gave bread to the carp, handed to us by the butler—small square pieces of bread in a straw basket. It was funny to see the fish appear as soon as the window was opened—some of them were enormous and very old. It seems they live to a great age; a guardian of the Palace at Fontainebleau always shows one to tourists, who is supposed to have been fed by the Emperor Napoleon. Those of Pinon knew all about it, lifting their brown heads out of the water and never missing their piece of bread.

We went back to the drawing-room for coffee, passing through the billiard room, where there are some good pictures. A fine life-size portrait of General Moreau (father of Mme. de Courval) in uniform, by Gerard—near it a trophy of four flags—Austrian, Saxon, Bavarian, and Hungarian—taken by the General; over the trophy three or four "lames d'honneur" (presentation swords) with name and inscription. There are also some pretty women's portraits in pastel—very delicate colours in old-fashioned oval frames—quite charming.

The drawing-room was a very handsome room also panelled in light gray carved wood; the furniture rather heavy and massive, curtains and coverings of thick, bright flowered velvet, but it looked suitable in that high old-fashioned room—light modern furniture would have been out of place.

As soon as we had finished our coffee we went for a walk—not the two old ladies, who settled down at once to their embroidery frames; one of them showed me her work—really quite beautiful—a church ornament of some kind, a painted Madonna on a ground of white satin; she was covering the whole ground with heavy gold embroidery, so thick it looked like mosaic.

The park is splendid, a real domain, all the paths and alleys beautifully kept and every description of tree—M. de Courval was always trying experiments with foreign trees and shrubs and apparently most successfully. I think the park would have been charming in its natural state, as there was a pretty little river running through the grounds and some tangles of bushes and rocks that looked quite wild—it might have been in the middle of the forest but everything had been done to assist nature. There were a "pièce d'eau," cascades, little bridges thrown over the river in picturesque spots, and on the highest point a tower (donjon), which was most effective, looked quite the old feudal towers of which so few remain now. They were used as watch towers, as a sentinel posted on the top could see a great distance over the plains and give warning of the approach of the enemy. As the day was fine—no mist—we had a beautiful view from the top, seeing plainly the great round tower of Coucy, the finest ruin in France—the others made out quite well the towers of the Laon Cathedral, but those I couldn't distinguish, seeing merely a dark spot on the horizon which might have been a passing cloud.

Coming back we crossed the "Allée des Soupirs," which has its legend like so many others in this country: It was called the "Allée des Soupirs" on account of the tragedy that took place there. The owner of the château at that time—a Comte de Lamothe—discovered his wife on too intimate terms with his great friend and her cousin; they fought in the Allée, and the Comte de Lamothe was killed by his friend. The widow tried to brave it out and lived on for some time at the château; but she was accursed and an evil spell on the place—everything went wrong and the château finally burnt down. The place was then sold to the de Courval family.

At the end of an hour the Marquise had had enough; I should not think she was much of a walker; she was struggling along in high-heeled shoes and proposed that she and I should return to the house and she would show me her atelier. W. and Mme. de Courval continued their tour of inspection which was to finish at the Home Farm, where she wanted to show him some small Breton cows which had just arrived. The atelier was a charming room; panelled like all the others in a light grey wood. One hardly saw the walls, for they were covered with pictures, engravings and a profusion of mirrors in gilt oval frames. It was evidently a favourite haunt of the Marquise's: books, papers and painting materials scattered about; the piano open and quantities of music on the music-stand; miniatures, snuff-boxes and little old-fashioned bibelots on all the tables, and an embroidery frame, of course, in one of the windows, near it a basket filled with bright coloured silks. The miniatures were, almost all, portraits of de Courvals of every age and in every possible costume: shepherdesses, court ladies of the time of Louis XV, La Belle Ferronnière with the jewel on her forehead, men in armour with fine, strongly marked faces; they must have been a handsome race. It is a pity there is no son to carry on the name. One daughter-in-law had no children; the other one, born an American, Mary Ray of New York, had only one daughter, the present Princesse de Poix, to whom Pinon now belongs.

We played a little; four hands—the classics, of course. All French women of that generation who played at all were brought up on strictly classical music. She had a pretty, delicate, old-fashioned touch; her playing reminded me of Madame A.'s.

When it was too dark to see any more we sat by the fire and talked till the others came in. She asked a great deal about my new life in Paris—feared I would find it stiff and dull after the easy happy family life I had been accustomed to. I said it was very different, of course, but there was much that was interesting, only I did not know the people well enough yet to appreciate the stories they were always telling about each other, also that I had made several "gaffes" quite innocently. I told her one which amused her very much, though she could not imagine how I ever could have said it. It was the first year of my marriage; we were dining in an Orleanist house, almost all the company Royalists and intimate friends of the Orléans Princes, and three or four moderate, *very* moderate Republicans like us. It was the 20th of January and the women were all talking about a ball they were going to the next night, 21st of January (anniversary of the death of Louis XVI).

They supposed they must wear mourning—such a bore. Still, on account of the Comtesse de Paris and the Orléans family generally, they thought they must do it—upon which I asked, really very much astonished: "On account of the Orléans family? but did not the Duc d'Orléans vote the King's execution?" There was an awful silence and then M. Leon Say, one of the cleverest and most delightful men of his time, remarked, with a twinkle in his eye: "Ma foi; je crois que Mme. Waddington a raison." There was a sort of nervous laugh and the conversation was changed. W. was much annoyed with me, "a foreigner so recently married, throwing down the gauntlet in that way." I assured him I had no purpose of any kind—I merely said what I thought, which is evidently unwise.

Mme. de Chaponay said she was afraid I would find it very difficult sometimes. French people—in society at least—were so excited against the Republic, anti-religious feeling, etc. "It must be very painful for you." "I don't think so; you see I am American, Republican and a Protestant; my point of view must be very different from that of a Frenchwoman and a Catholic." She was very charming, however; intelligent, cultivated, speaking beautiful French with a pretty carefully trained voice—English just as well; we spoke the two languages going from one to the other without knowing why. I was quite sorry when we were summoned to tea. The room looked so pretty in the twilight, the light from the fire danced all over the pictures and gilt frames of the mirrors, leaving the corners quite in shadow. The curtains were not drawn and we saw the darkness creeping up over the lawn; quite at the edge of the wood the band of white mist was rising, which we love to see in our part of the country, as it always means a fine day for the morrow.

We had a cheery tea. W. and Mme. de Courval had made a long "tournée," and W. quite approved of all the changes and new acquisitions she had made, particularly the little Breton cows. We left rather hurriedly as we had just time to catch our train.

Our last glimpse of the château as we looked back from the turn in the avenue was charming; there were lights in almost all the windows, which were reflected in the moat; the moon was rising over the woods at the back, and every tower and cornice of the enormous pile stood out sharply in the cold clear light.

We didn't move often once we were settled in the château for the autumn. It was very difficult to get W. away from his books and coins and his woods; but occasionally a shooting party tempted him. We went sometimes, about the Toussaint when the leaves were nearly fallen, to stay with friends who had a fine château and estate about three hours by rail from Paris, in the midst of the great plains of the Aube. The first time we went, soon after my marriage, I was rather doubtful as to how I should like it. I had never stayed in a French country house and imagined it would be very stiff and formal; however, the invitation was for three days—two days of shooting and one of rest—and I thought that I could get through without being too homesick.

We arrived about 4.30 for tea; the journey from Paris was through just the same uninteresting country one always sees when leaving by the Gare de l'Est. I think it is the ugliest sortie of all Paris. As we got near the château the Seine appeared, winding in and out of the meadows in very leisurely fashion. We just saw the house from the train, standing rather low. The station is at the park gates—in fact, the railway and the canal run through the property. Two carriages were waiting (we were not the only guests), and a covered cart for the maids and baggage. A short drive through a fine avenue of big trees skirting broad lawns brought us to the house, which looked very imposing with its long façade and rows of lighted windows. We drove through arcades covered with ivy into a very large court-yard, the château stables and communs taking three sides. There was a pièce d'eau at one end, a colombier at the other. There was no perron or stately entrance; in one corner a covered porch, rather like what one sees in England, shut in with glass door and windows and filled with plants, a good many chrysanthemums, which made a great mass of colour. The hall doors were wide open as the carriage drove up, Monsieur A. and his wife waiting for us just inside, Mme. A. his mother, the mistress of the château, at the door of the salon. We went into a large, high hall, well lighted, a bright fire burning, plenty of servants. It looked most cheerful and comfortable on a dark November afternoon. We left our wraps in the hall, and went straight into the drawing-room. I have been there so often since that I hardly remember my first impression. It was a corner room, high ceiling, big windows, and fine tapestries on the walls; some of them with a pink ground (very unusual), and much envied and admired by all art collectors. Mme. A. told me she found them all rolled up in a bundle in the garret when she married. A tea-table was standing before the sofa, and various people working and having their tea. We were not a large party—Comte and Comtesse de B. (she a daughter of the house) and three or four men, deputies and senators, all political. They counted eight guns. We sat there about half an hour, then there was a general move, and young Mme. A. showed us our rooms, which were most comfortable, fires burning, lamps lighted. She told us dinner was at 7.30; the first bell would ring at seven. I was the only lady besides the family. I told my maid to ask some of the others what their mistresses were going to wear. She said ordinary evening dress, with natural flowers in their hair, and that I would receive a small bouquet, which I did, only as I never wear anything in my hair, I put them on my corsage, which did just as well.

The dinner was pleasant, the dining-room a fine, large hall (had been stables) with a fireplace at each end, and big windows giving on the court-yard. It was so large that the dinner table (we were fourteen) seemed lost in space. The talk was almost exclusively political and amusing enough. All the men were, or had been, deputies, and every possible question was discussed. Mme. A. was charming, very intelligent, and animated, having lived all her life with clever people, and having taken part in all the changes that France has gone through in the last fifty years. She had been a widow for about two years when I first stayed there, and it was pretty to see her children with her. Her two sons, one married, the other a young officer, were so respectful and fond of their mother, and her daughter perfectly devoted to her.

The men all went off to smoke after coffee, and we women were left to ourselves for quite a long time. The three ladies all had work—knitting or crochet—

and were making little garments, brassieres, and petticoats for all the village children. They were quite surprised that I had nothing and said they would teach me to crochet. The evening was not very long after the men came back. Some remained in the billiard-room, which opens out of the salon, and played cochonnet, a favourite French game. We heard violent discussions as to the placing of the balls, and some one asked for a yard measure, to be quite sure the count was correct. Before we broke up M. A. announced the programme for the next day. Breakfast for all the men at eight o'clock in the dining-room, and an immediate start for the woods; luncheon at the Pavilion d'Hiver at twelve in the woods, the ladies invited to join the shooters and follow one or two battues afterward. It was a clear, cold night, and there seemed every prospect of a beautiful day for the battues.

The next morning was lovely. I went to my maid's room, just across the corridor to see the motors start. All our rooms looked out on the park, and on the other side of the corridor was a succession of small rooms giving on the courtyard, which were always kept for the maids and valets of the guests. It was an excellent arrangement, for in some of the big châteaux, where the servants were at the top of the house, or far off in another wing, communications were difficult. There were two carriages and a sort of tapissière following with guns, servants, and cartridges. I had a message from Mme. A. asking if I had slept well, and sending me the paper; and a visit from Comtesse de B. who, I think, was rather anxious about my garments. She had told me the night before that the ploughed fields were something awful, and hoped I had brought short skirts and thick boots. I think the sight of my short Scotch homespun skirt and high boots reassured her. We started about 11.30 in an open carriage with plenty of furs and wraps. It wasn't really very cold—just a nice nip in the air, and no wind. We drove straight into the woods from the park. There is a beautiful green alley which faces one just going out of the gate, but it was too steep to mount in a carriage. The woods are very extensive, the roads not too bad—considering the season, extremely well kept. Every now and then through an opening in the trees we had a pretty view over the plains. As we got near the pavilion we heard shots not very far off—evidently the shooters were getting hungry and coming our way. It was a pretty rustic scene as we arrived. The pavilion, a log house, standing in a clearing, alleys branching off in every direction, a horse and cart which had brought the provisions from the château tied to one of the trees. It was shut in on three sides, wide open in front, a bright fire burning and a most appetizing table spread. Just outside another big fire was burning, the cook waiting for the first sportsman to appear to begin his classic dishes, omelette au lard and ragoât de mouton. I was rather hungry and asked for a piece of the pain de ménage they had for the traqueurs (beaters). I like the brown country bread so much better than the little rolls and crisp loaves most people ask for in France. Besides our own breakfast there was an enormous pot on the fire with what looked like an excellent substantial soup for the men. In a few minutes the party arrived; first the shooters, each man carrying his gun; then the game cart, which looked very well garnished, an army of beaters bringing up the rear. They made quite a picturesque group, all dressed in white. There have been so many accidents in some of the big shoots, people imprudently firing at something moving in the bushes, which proved to be a man and not a roebuck, that M.

A. dresses all his men in white. The gentlemen were very cheerful, said they had had capital sport, and were quite ready for their breakfast. We didn't linger very long at table, as the days were shortening fast, and we wanted to follow some of the battues. The beaters had their breakfast while we were having ours—were all seated on the ground around a big kettle of soup, with huge hunks of brown bread on their tin plates.

We started off with the shooters. Some walking, some driving, and had one pretty battue of rabbits; after that two of pheasants, which were most amusing. There were plenty of birds, and they came rocketing over our heads in fine style. I found that Comtesse de B. was quite right about the necessity for short skirts and thick boots. We stood on the edge of a ploughed field, which we had to cross afterward on our way home, and I didn't think it was possible to have such cakes of mud as we had on our boots. We scraped off some with sticks, but our boots were so heavy with what remained that the walk home was tiring.

Mme. A. was standing at the hall-door when we arrived, and requested us not to come into the hall, but to go in by the lingerie entrance and up the back stairs, so I fancy we hadn't got much dirt off. I had a nice rest until 4.30, when I went down to the salon for tea. We had all changed our outdoor garments and got into rather smart day dresses (none of those ladies wore tea-gowns). The men appeared about five; some of them came into the salon notwithstanding their muddy boots, and then came the livre de chasse and the recapitulation of the game, which is always most amusing. Everyman counted more pieces than his beater had found.

The dinner and evening were pleasant, the guests changing a little. Two of the original party went off before dinner, two others arrived, one of them a Cabinet minister (Finances). He was very clever and defended himself well when his policy was freely criticised. While we women were alone after dinner, Mme. A. showed me how to make crochet petticoats. She gave me a crochet-needle and some wool and had wonderful patience, for it seemed a most arduous undertaking to me, and all my rows were always crooked; however, I did learn, and have made hundreds since. All the children in our village pull up their little frocks and show me their crochet petticoats whenever we meet them. They are delighted to have them, for those we make are of good wool (not laine de bienfaisance, which is stiff and coarse), and last much longer than those one buys.

The second day was quite different. There was no shooting. We were left to our own devices until twelve o'clock breakfast. W. and I went for a short stroll in the park. We met M. A., who took us over the farm, all so well ordered and prosperous. After breakfast we had about an hour of salon before starting for the regular tournée de propriétaire through park and gardens. The three ladies—Mme. A., her daughter, and daughter-in-law—had beautiful work. Mme. A. was making portières for her daughter's room, a most elaborate pattern, reeds and high plants, a very large piece of work; the other two had also very complicated work—one a table-cover, velvet, heavily embroidered, the other a church ornament (almost all the Frenchwomen of a certain monde turn their wedding dresses, usually of white satin, into a priest's vêtement). The Catholic priests have all sorts of vestments which they wear on different occasions; purple in Lent, red on any martyr's fête, white for all the fêtes of the Virgin. Some of the churches are very rich with chasubles and altar-cloths trimmed with fine old lace, which have been given to them. It looks funny sometimes to see a very ordinary country curé, a farmer's son, with a heavy peasant face, wearing one of those delicate white-satin chasubles.

Before starting to join the shooters at breakfast Mme. A. took me all over the house. It is really a beautiful establishment, very large, and most comfortable. Quantities of pictures and engravings, and beautiful Empire furniture. There is quite a large chapel at the end of the corridor on the ground-floor, where they have mass every Sunday. The young couple have a charming installation, really a small house, in one of the wings—bedrooms, dressing-rooms, boudoir, cabinet de travail, and a separate entrance—so that M. A. can receive any one who comes to see him on business without having them pass through the château. Mme. A. has her rooms on the ground-floor at the other end of the house. Her sitting-room with glass door opens into a winter garden filled with plants, which gives on the park; her bedroom is on the other side, looking on the court-yard; a large library next it, light and space everywhere, plenty of servants, everything admirably arranged.

The evening mail goes out at 7.30, and every evening at seven exactly the letter-carrier came down the corridor knocking at all the doors and asking for letters. He had stamps, too, at least *French* stamps. I could never get a foreign stamp (twenty-five centimes)—had to put one of fifteen and two of five when I had a foreign letter. I don't really think there were any in the country. I don't believe they had a foreign correspondent of any description. It was a thoroughly French establishment of the best kind.

We walked about the small park and gardens in the afternoon. The gardens are enormous; one can drive through them. Mme. A. drove in her pony carriage. They still had some lovely late roses which filled me with envy—ours were quite finished.

The next day was not quite so fine, gray and misty, but a good shooting day, no wind. We joined the gentlemen for lunch in another pavilion farther away and rather more open than the one of the other day. However, we were warm enough with our coats on, a good fire burning, and hot bricks for our feet. The battues (aux échelles) that day were quite a new experience for me. I had never seen anything like it. The shooters were placed in a semicircle, not very far apart. Each man was provided with a high double ladder. The men stood on the top (the women seated themselves on the rungs of the ladders and hung on as well as they could). I went the first time with W., and he made me so many recommendations that I was quite nervous. I mustn't sit too high up or I would gêner him, as he was obliged to shoot down for the rabbits; and I mustn't sit too near the ground, or I might get a shot in the ankles from one of the other men. I can't say it was an absolute pleasure. The seat (if seat it could be called) was anything but comfortable, and the detonation of the gun just over my head was decidedly trying; still it was a novelty, and if the other women could stand it I could.

For the second battue I went with Comte de B. That was rather worse, for he shot much oftener than W., and I was quite distracted with the noise of the gun. We were nearer the other shooters, too, and I fancied their aim was very near my ankles. It was a pretty view from the top of the ladder. I climbed up when the battues were over. We looked over the park and through the trees, quite bare and stripped of their leaves, on the great plains, with hardly a break of wood or hills, stretching away to the horizon. The ground was thickly carpeted with red and yellow leaves, little columns of smoke rising at intervals where people were burning weeds or rotten wood in the fields; and just enough purple mist to poetize everything. B. is a very careful shot. I was with him the first day at a rabbit battue where we were placed rather near each other, and every man was asked to keep quite to his own place and to shoot straight before him. After one or two shots B. stepped back and gave his gun to his servant. I asked what was the matter. He showed me the man next, evidently not used to shooting, who was walking up and down, shooting in every direction, and as fast as he could cram the cartridges into his gun. So he stepped back into the alley and waited until the battue was over.

The party was much smaller that night at dinner. Every one went away but W. and me. The talk was most interesting—all about the war, the first days of the Assemblée Nationale at Bordeaux, and the famous visit of the Comte de Chambord to Versailles, when the Maréchal de MacMahon, President of the Republic, refused to see him. I told them of my first evening visit to Mme. Thiers, the year I was married. Mme. Thiers lived in a big gloomy house in the Place St. Georges, and received every evening. M. Thiers, who was a great worker all his life and a very early riser, always took a nap at the end of the day. The ladies (Mlle. Dosne, a sister of Mme. Thiers, lived with them) unfortunately had not that good habit. They took their little sleep after dinner. We arrived there (it was a long way from us, we lived near the Arc de l'Étoile) one evening a little before ten. There were already four or five men, no ladies. We were shown into a large drawing-room, M. Thiers standing with his back to the fireplace, the centre of a group of black coats. He was very amiable, said I would find Mme. Thiers in a small salon just at the end of the big one; told W. to join their group, he had something to say to him, and I passed on. I did find Mme. Thiers and Mlle. Dosne in the small salon at the other end, both asleep, each in an arm-chair. I was really embarrassed. They didn't hear me coming in, and were sleeping quite happily and comfortably. I didn't like to go back to the other salon, where there were only men, so I sat down on a sofa and looked about me, and tried to feel as if it was quite a natural occurrence to be invited to come in the evening and to find my hostess asleep. After a few minutes I heard the swish of a satin dress coming down the big salon and a lady appeared, very handsome and well dressed, whom I didn't know at all. She evidently was accustomed to the state of things; she looked about her smilingly, then came up to me, called me by name, and introduced herself, Mme. A. the wife of an admiral whom I often met afterward. She told me not to mind, there wasn't the slightest intention of rudeness, that both ladies would wake up in a few minutes quite unconscious of having really slept. We talked about ten minutes, not lowering our voices particularly. Suddenly Mme. Thiers opened her eyes, was wide awake at once—how quietly we must have come in; she had only just closed her eyes for a moment, the lights tired her, etc. Mlle. Dosne said the same thing, and then we went on talking easily enough. Several more ladies came in, but only two or three men. *They* all remained in the farther room talking, or rather listening, to M. Thiers. He was already a very old man, and when he began to talk no one interrupted him; it was almost a monologue. I went back several times to the Place St. Georges, but took good care to go later, so that the ladies should have their nap over. One of the young diplomat's wives had the same experience, rather worse, for when the ladies woke up they didn't know her. She was very shy, spent a wretched ten minutes before they woke, and was too nervous to name herself. She was half crying when her husband came to the rescue.

We left the next morning early, as W. had people coming to him in the afternoon. I enjoyed my visit thoroughly, and told them afterward of my misgivings and doubts as to how I should get along with strangers for two or three days. I think they had rather the same feeling. They were very old friends of my husband's, and though they received me charmingly from the first, it brought a foreign and new element into their circle.

Another interesting old château, most picturesque, with towers, moat, and drawbridge, is Lorrey-le-Bocage, belonging to the Comte de S. It stands very well, in a broad moat—the water clear and rippling and finishing in a pretty little stream that runs off through the meadows. The place is beautifully kept—gardens, lawns, courts, in perfect order. It has no particular *historic* interest for the family, having been bought by the parents of the present owner.

I was there, the first time, in very hot weather, the 14th of July (the French National fête commemorating the fall of the Bastille). I went for a stroll in the park the morning after I arrived, but I collapsed under a big tree at once—hadn't the energy to move. Everything looked so hot and not a breath of air anywhere. The moat looked glazed—so absolutely still under the bright summer sun—big flies were buzzing and skimming over the surface, and the flowers and plants were drooping in their beds.

Inside it was delightful, the walls so thick that neither heat nor cold could penetrate. The house is charming. The big drawing-room—where we always sat—was a large, bright room with windows on each side and lovely views over park and gardens; and all sorts of family portraits and souvenirs dating from Louis XV to the Comte de Paris. The men of the family—all ardent Royalists—have been, for generations, distinguished as soldiers and statesmen.

One of them—a son of the famous Maréchal de S, brought up in the last years of the reign of Louis XV—carried his youthful ardour and dreams of liberty to America and took part, as did so many of the young French nobles, in the great struggle for independence that was being fought out on the other side of the Atlantic. Soon after his return to France he was named Ambassador to Russia to the court of Catherine II, and was supposed to have been very much in the good graces of that very pleasure-loving sovereign. He accompanied her on her famous trip to the Crimea, arranged for her by her minister and favourite, Potemkin—when fairy villages, with happy populations singing and dancing, sprang up in the road wherever she passed as if by magic—quite dispelling her ideas of the poverty and oppression of some of her subjects.

Among the portraits there is a miniature of the Empress Catherine. It is a fine, strongly marked face. She wears a high fur cap—a sort of military pelisse with lace jabots and diamond star. The son of the Maréchal, also soldier and courtier, was aide-de-camp to Napoleon and made almost all his campaigns with him. His description of the Russian campaign and the retreat of the "Grande Armée" from Moscow is one of the most graphic and interesting that has ever been written of those awful days. His memoirs are quite charming. Childhood and early youth passed in the country in all the agonies of the Terror—simply and severely brought up in an atmosphere absolutely hostile to any national or popular movement.

The young student, dreaming of a future and regeneration for France, arrived one day in Paris, where an unwonted stir denoted that something was going on. He heard and saw the young Republican General Bonaparte addressing some regiments. He marked the proud bearing of the men—even the recruits—and in an explosion of patriotism his vocation was decided. He enlisted at once in the Republican ranks. It was a terrible decision to confide to his family, and particularly to his grandfather, the old Maréchal de S. a glorious veteran of many campaigns and an ardent Royalist. His father approved, although it was a terrible falling off from all the lessons and examples of his family—but it was a difficult confession to make to the Maréchal. I will give the scene in his own words (translated, of course—the original is in French).

"I was obliged to return to Châlenoy to relate my 'coup-de-tête' to my grandfather. I arrived early in the morning and approached his bed in the most humble attitude. He said to me, very sharply, 'You have been unfaithful to all the traditions of your ancestors—but it is done. Remember that you have enlisted voluntarily in the Republican army; serve it frankly and loyally, for your decision is made, you cannot now go back on it.' Then seeing the tears running down my cheeks (he too was moved), and taking my hand with the only one he had left, he drew me to him and pressed me on his heart. Then giving me seventy louis (it was all he had), he added, 'This will help you to complete your equipment—go, and at least carry bravely and faithfully, under the flag it has pleased you to choose, the name you bear and the honour of your family.'"

The present Count, too, has played a part in politics in these troublous times, when decisions were almost as hard to take, and one was torn between the desire to do something for one's country and the difficulty of detaching oneself from old traditions and memories. People whose grandfathers have died on the scaffold can hardly be expected to be enthusiastic about the Republic and the Marseillaise. Yet if the nation wants the Republic, and every election accentuates that opinion, it is very difficult to fight against the current.

When I first married, just after the Franco-Prussian War, there seemed some chance of the moderate men, on both sides, joining in a common effort against the radical movement, putting themselves at the head of it and in that way directing and controlling—but very soon the different sections in parliament defined themselves so sharply that any sort of compromise was difficult. My host was named deputy, immediately after the war, and though by instinct, training, and association a Royalist and a personal friend of the Orléans family, he was one of a small group of liberal-patriotic deputies who might have supported loyally a moderate Republic had the other Republicans not made their position untenable. There was an instinctive, unreasonable distrust of any of the old families whose names and antecedents had kept them apart from any republican movement.

We had pleasant afternoons in the big drawing-room. In the morning we did what we liked. The Maîtresse de Maison never appeared in the drawing-room till the twelve o'clock breakfast. I used to see her from my window, coming and going—sometimes walking, when she was making the round of the farm and garden, oftener in her little pony carriage and occasionally in the automobile of her niece, who was staying in the house. She occupied herself very much with all the village—old people and children, everybody. After breakfast we used to sit sometimes in the drawing-room—the two ladies working, the Comte de S. reading his paper and telling us anything interesting he found there. Both ladies had most artistic work—Mme. de S. a church ornament, white satin ground with raised flowers and garlands, stretched, of course, on the large embroidery frames they all use. Her niece, Duchesse d'E., had quite another "installation" in one of the windows—a table with all sorts of delicate little instruments. She was book-binding—doing quite lovely things in imitation of the old French binding. It was a work that required most delicate manipulation, but she seemed to do it quite easily. I was rather humiliated with my little knit petticoats—very hot work it is on a blazing July day.

III

THE HOME OF LAFAYETTE

La Grange was looking its loveliest when I arrived the other day. It was a bright, beautiful October afternoon and the first glimpse of the château was most picturesque. It was all the more striking as the run down from Paris was so ugly and commonplace. The suburbs of Paris around the Gare de l'Est—the Plain of St. Denis and all the small villages, with kitchen gardens, rows of green vegetables under glass "cloches"—are anything but interesting. It was not until we got near Gréty and alongside of Ferrières, the big Rothschild place, that we seemed to be in the country. The broad green alleys of the park, with the trees just changing a little, were quite charming. Our station was Verneuil l'Etang, a quiet little country station dumped down in the middle of the fields, and a drive of about fifty minutes brought us to the château. The country is not at all pretty, always the same thing—great cultivated fields stretching off on each side of the road—every now and then a little wood or clump of trees. One does not see the château from the high road.

We turned off sharply to the left and at the end of a long avenue saw the house, half hidden by the trees. The entrance through a low archway, flanked on each side by high round towers covered with ivy, is most picturesque. The château is built around three sides of a square court-yard, the other side looking straight over broad green meadows ending in a background of wood. A moat runs almost all around the house—a border of salvias making a belt of colour which is most effective. We found the family—Marquis and Marquise de Lasteyrie and their two sons—waiting at the hall door. The Marquis, great-grandson of the General Marquis de Lafayette, is a type of the well-born, courteous French gentleman (one of the most attractive types, to my mind, that one can meet anywhere). There is something in perfectly well-bred French people of a certain class that one never sees in any other nationality. Such refinement and charm of manner—a great desire to put every one at their ease and to please the person with whom they are thrown for the moment. That, after all, is all one cares for in the casual acquaintances one makes in society. From friends, of course, we want something deeper and more lasting, but life is too short to find out the depth and sterling qualities of the world in general.

The Marquise is an Englishwoman, a cousin of her husband, their common ancestor being the Duke of Leinster; clever, cultivated, hospitable, and very large minded, which has helped her very much in her married life in France during our troubled epoch, when religious questions and political discussions do so much to embitter personal relations. The two sons are young and gay, doing the honours of their home simply and with no pose of any kind. There were two English couples staying in the house.

We had tea in the dining-room downstairs—a large room with panels and chimney-piece of dark carved wood. Two portraits of men in armour stand out well from the dark background. There is such a wealth of pictures, engravings, and tapestries all over the house that one cannot take it all in at first. The two drawing-rooms on the first floor are large and comfortable, running straight through the house; the end room in the tower—a round room with windows on all sides—quite charming. The contrast between the modern—English—comforts (low, wide chairs, writing-table, rugs, cushions, and centre-table covered with books in all languages, a very rare thing in a French château, picture papers, photographs, etc.) and the straight-backed, spindle-legged old furniture and stiff, old-fashioned ladies and gentlemen, looking down from their heavy gold frames, is very attractive. There is none of the formality and look of not being lived in which one sees in so many French salons, and yet it is not at all modern. One never loses for a moment the feeling of being in an old château-fort.

It was so pretty looking out of my bedroom window this morning. It was a bright, beautiful autumn day, the grass still quite green. Some of the trees changing a little, the yellow leaves quite golden in the sun. There are many American trees in the park—a splendid Virginia Creeper, and a Gloire de Dijon rose-bush, still full of bloom, were sprawling over the old gray walls. Animals of all kinds were walking about the court-yard; some swans and a lame duck, which had wandered up from the moat, standing on the edge and looking about with much interest; a lively little fox-terrier, making frantic dashes at nothing; one of the sons starting for a shoot with gaiters and game-bag, and his gun over his shoulder, his dog at his heels expectant and eager. Some of the guests were strolling about and from almost all the windows—wide open to let in the warm morning sun—there came cheerful greetings.

I went for a walk around the house before breakfast. There are five large round towers covered with ivy—the walls extraordinarily thick—the narrow little slits for shooting with arrows and the round holes for cannon balls tell their own story of rough feudal life. On one side of the castle there is a large hole in the wall, made by a cannon ball sent by Turenne. He was passing one day and asked to whom the château belonged. On hearing that the owner was the Maréchal de la Feuillade, one of his political adversaries, he sent a cannon ball as a souvenir of his passage, and the gap has never been filled up.

I went all over the house later with the Marquis de Lasteyrie. Of course, what interested me most was Lafayette's private apartments—bedroom and library—the latter left precisely as it was during Lafayette's lifetime; bookcases filled with his books in their old-fashioned bindings, running straight around the walls and a collection of manuscripts and autograph letters from kings and queens of France and most of the celebrities of the days of the Valois—among them several letters from Catherine de Medicis, Henry IV, and la Reine Margot. One curious one from Queen Margot in which she explains to the Vicomte de Chabot (ancestor of my host) that she was very much preoccupied in looking out for a wife for him with a fine dot, but that it was always difficult to find a rich heiress for a poor seigneur.

There are also autographs of more modern days, among which is a letter from an English prince to the Vicomte de Chabot (grandfather of the Marquis de Lasteyrie), saying that he loses no time in telling him of the birth of a very fine little girl. He certainly never realized when he wrote that letter what would be the future of his baby daughter. The writer was the Duke of Kent—the fine little girl, Queen Victoria.

In a deep window-seat in one corner, overlooking the farm, is the writing-table of Lafayette. In the drawers are preserved several books of accounts, many of the items being in his handwriting. Also his leather arm-chair (which was exhibited at the Chicago World's Fair), and a horn or speaking-trumpet through which he gave his orders to the farm hands from the window. The library opened into his bedroom—now the boudoir of the Marquise de Lasteyrie—with a fine view over moat and meadow. In this room there have been many changes, but the old doors of carved oak still remain.

There are many interesting family portraits—one of the father of Lafayette, killed at Minden, leaving his young son to be brought up by two aunts, whose portraits are on either side of the fireplace.

It is curious to see the two portraits of the same epoch so absolutely unlike. Mme. de Chavagnac, an old lady, very simply dressed, almost Puritanical, with a white muslin fichu over her plain black silk dress—the other, Mademoiselle de Lafayette, in the court dress of the time of Louis XVI, pearls and roses in the high, powdered coiffure and a bunch of orange flowers on one shoulder, to indicate that she was not a married woman.

There were pictures and souvenirs of all the Orléans family—the Lasteyries having been always faithful and devoted friends of those unfortunate princes; a charming engraving of the Comte de Paris, a noble looking boy in all the bravery of white satin and feathers—the original picture is in the possession of the Duc de Chartres. It was sad to realize when one looked at the little prince with his bright eyes and proud bearing, that the end of his life would be so melancholy—exile and death in a foreign land.

There are all sorts of interesting pictures and engravings scattered about the house in the numberless corridors and anterooms. One most interesting and very rare print represents a review at Potsdam held by Frederick the Great. Two conspicuous figures are the young Marquis de Lafayette in powdered wig and black silk ribbon, and the English General Lord Cornwallis, destined to meet as adversaries many years later during the American Revolution. There are many family pictures on the great stone staircase, both French and English, the Marquis de Lasteyrie, on the maternal side, being a great-grandson of the Duke of Leinster. Some of the English portraits are very charming, quite different from the French pictures.

In the centre panel is the well-known portrait of Lafayette by Ary Scheffer—not in uniform—no trace of the dashing young soldier; a middle-aged man in a long fur coat, hat and stick in his hand; looking, as one can imagine he did when he settled down, after his brilliant and eventful career, to the simple patriarchal life at La Grange, surrounded by devoted children, grandchildren, and friends.

We were interrupted long before I had seen all the interesting part of the house and its contents, as it was time to start for La Houssaye, where all the party were expected at tea. We went off in three carriages—quite like a "noce," as the Marquise remarked. The drive (about an hour) was not particularly interesting. We were in the heart of the great agricultural district and drove through kilometres of planted fields—no hills and few woods.

We came rather suddenly on the château, which stands low, like all châteaux surrounded by moats, turning directly from the little village into the park, which is beautifully laid out with fine old trees. We had glimpses of a lovely garden as we drove up to the house, and of two old towers—one round and one square. The château stands well—a very broad moat, almost a river, running straight around the house and gardens. We crossed the drawbridge, which always gives me a sensation of old feudal times and recalls the days of my childhood when I used to sit under the sickle-pear tree at "Cherry Lawn" reading Scott's "Marmion"—"Up drawbridge, grooms—what, Warder, ho! Let the portcullis fall!" wondering what a "portcullis" was, and if I should ever see one or even a château-fort.

La Houssaye is an old castle built in the eleventh century, but has passed through many vicissitudes. All that remains of the original building are the towers and the foundations. It was restored in the sixteenth century and has since remained unchanged. During the French Revolution the family of the actual proprietor installed themselves in one of the towers and lived there many long weary weeks, never daring to venture out, show any lights, or give any sign of life—in daily terror of being discovered and dragged to Paris before the dreaded revolutionary tribunals. Later it was given, by Napoleon, to the Marshall Augereau, who died there. It has since been in the family of the present proprietor, Monsieur de Mimont, who married an American, Miss Forbes.

The rain, which had been threatening all the afternoon, came down in torrents just as we crossed the drawbridge, much to the disappointment of our host and hostess, who were anxious to show us their garden, which is famous in all the countryside. However, in spite of the driving rain, we caught glimpses through the windows of splendid parterres of salvias and cannas, making great spots of colour in a beautiful bit of smooth green lawn. In old days the château was much bigger, stretching out to the towers. Each successive proprietor has diminished the buildings, and the present château, at the back, stands some little distance from the moat, the vacant space being now transformed into their beautiful gardens.

We only saw the ground-floor of the house, which is most comfortable. We left our wraps in the large square hall and passed through one drawing-room and a small library into another, which is charming—a corner room looking on the gardens—the walls, panels of light gray wood, prettily carved with wreaths and flowers.

We had tea in the dining-room on the other side of the hall; a curious room, rather, with red brick walls and two old narrow doors of carved oak. The tea—

most abundant—was very acceptable after our long damp drive. One dish was rather a surprise—American waffles—not often to be found, I imagine, in an old French feudal castle, but Madame de Mimont's nationality explained it. I was very sorry not to see the park which is beautifully laid out, but the rain was falling straight down as hard as it could—almost making waves in the moat, and a curtain of mist cut off the end of the park.

Our dinner and evening at La Grange were delightful. The dining-room is particularly charming at night. The flowers on the table, this evening, were red, and the lights from the handsome silver candélabres made a brilliant spot of warmth and colour against the dark panelled walls—just shining on the armour of the fine Ormond portraits hanging on each side of the fireplace. The talk was always easy and pleasant.

One of the guests, the naval attache to the British Embassy to France, had been "en mission" at Madrid at the time of the Spanish Royal marriage. The balcony of the English Embassy overlooked the spot where the bomb was thrown. In eighty-five seconds from the time they heard the detonation (in the first second they thought it was a salute), the Ambassador, followed by his suite, was at the door of the royal carriage. He said the young sovereigns looked very pale but calm; the king, perhaps, more agitated than the Queen.

We finished the evening with music and dumb crambo—that particularly English form of amusement, which I have never seen well done except by English people. It always fills me with astonishment whenever I see it. It is so at variance with the English character. They are usually so very shy and self-conscious. One would never believe they could throw themselves into this really childish game with so much entrain. The performance is simple enough. Some of the company retire from the drawing-room; those who remain choose a word—chair, hat, cat, etc. This evening the word was "mat." We told the two actors—Mrs. P. and the son of the house—they must act (nothing spoken) a word which rhymed with *hat*. I will say they found it very quickly, but some of their attempts were funny enough—really very cleverly done. It amused me perfectly, though I must frankly confess I should have been incapable of either acting or guessing the word. The only one I made out was fat, when they both came in so stuffed out with pillows and bolsters as to be almost unrecognizable. The two dogs—a beautiful little fox-terrier and a fine collie—went nearly mad, barking and yapping every time the couple appeared—their excitement reaching a climax when the actors came in and stretched themselves out on each side of the door, having finally divined the word mat. The dogs made such frantic dashes at them that M. and Mme. de Lasteyrie had to carry them off bodily.

The next morning I went for a walk with M. de Lasteyrie. We strolled up and down the "Allée des Soupirs," so called in remembrance of one of the early chatelaines who trailed her mourning robes and widow's veil over the fallen leaves, bemoaning her solitude until a favoured suitor appeared on the scene and carried her away to his distant home—but the Allée still retains its name.

The park is small, but very well laid out. Many of the memoirs of the time speak of walks and talks with Lafayette under the beautiful trees.

During the last years of Lafayette's life, La Grange was a cosmopolitan centre. Distinguished people from all countries came there, anxious to see the great champion of liberty; among them many Americans, who always found a gracious, cordial welcome; one silent guest—a most curious episode which I will give in the words of the Marquis de Lasteyrie:

"One American, however, in Lafayette's own time, came on a lonely pilgrimage to La Grange; he was greeted with respect, but of that greeting he took no heed. He was a silent guest, nor has he left any record of his impressions; in fact, he was dead before starting on his journey. He arrived quite simply one fine autumn morning, in his coffin, accompanied by a letter which said: 'William Summerville, having the greatest admiration for the General Lafayette, begs he will bury him in his land at La Grange.' This, being against the law, could not be done, but Lafayette bought the whole of the small cemetery of the neighbouring village and laid the traveller from over the sea to rest in his ground indeed, though not under one of the many American trees at La Grange itself, of which the enthusiastic wanderer had probably dreamed."

They told me many interesting things, too long to write, about the last years of Lafayette's life spent principally at La Grange. A charming account of that time and the lavish hospitality of the château is given by Lady Morgan, in her well-known "Diary." Some of her descriptions are most amusing; the arrival, for instance, of Lady Holland at the home of the Republican General. "She is always preceded by a fourgon from London containing her own favourite meubles of Holland House—her bed, fauteuil, carpet, etc., and divers other articles too numerous to mention, but which enter into her Ladyship's superfluchoses très nécessaires, at least to a grande dame—one of her female attendants and a groom of the chambers precede her to make all ready for her reception. However, her original manner, though it startles the French ladies, amuses them."

Her Irish ladyship (Lady Morgan) seems to have been troubled by no shyness in asking questions of the General. She writes: "Is it true, General, I asked, that you once went to a bal masque at the opera with the Queen of France—Marie Antoinette—leaning on your arm, the King knowing nothing of the matter till her return? I am afraid so, said he. She was so indiscreet, and I can conscientiously add—so innocent. However, the Comte d'Artois was also of the party, and we were all young, enterprising, and pleasure-loving. But what is most absurd in the adventure was that, when I pointed out Mme. du Barry to her—whose figure and favourite domino I knew—the Queen expressed the most anxious desire to hear her speak and bade me intriguer her. She answered me flippantly, and I am sure if I had offered her my other arm, the Queen would not have objected to it. Such was the esprit d'aventure at that time in the court of Versailles and in the head of the haughty daughter of Austria."

I remember quite well the parents of my host. The Marquise, a type of the grande dame, with blue eyes and snow white hair survived her husband many years. During the war of 1870 they, like many other châtelains, had Prussian soldiers in their house. The following characteristic anecdote of the Marquise was told to me by her son:

"There are still to be seen at La Grange two little cannon which had been given to Lafayette by the Garde Nationale. One December morning, in 1870, when the house was full of German troops, Madame de Lasteyrie was awakened by a noise under the archway, and looking out of her window saw, in the dim light, the two guns being carried off by the German soldiers. In an instant, her bare feet hastily thrust into slippers, her hair like a long white mane hanging down her back, with a dressing gown thrown over her shoulders, she started in pursuit. She followed them about three miles and at last came upon them at the top of a hill. After much persuasion and after spiking the guns (in no case could they have done great damage), the soldiers were induced to give them up, and departed, leaving her alone in the frost and starlight waiting for the morning. She sat bare-footed (for she had lost her shoes) but triumphant on her small cannon in the deep snow till the day came and the farm people stole out and dragged them all—the old lady and the two guns—back to the house."

I was sorry to go—the old château, with its walls and towers soft and grey in the sunlight, seems to belong absolutely to another century. I felt as if I had been transported a hundred years back and had lived a little of the simple patriarchal life that made such a beautiful end to Lafayette's long and eventful career. The present owner keeps up the traditions of his grandfather. I was thinking last night what a cosmopolitan group we were. Three or four different nationalities, speaking alternately the two languages—French and English—many of the party having travelled all over the world and all interested in politics, literature, and music; in a different way, perhaps, but quite as much as the "belles dames et beaux esprits" of a hundred years ago. Everything changes as time goes on (I don't know if I would say that *everything* improves), but I carried away the same impression of a warm welcome and large hospitable life that every one speaks of who saw La Grange during Lafayette's life.

IV

WINTER AT THE CHATEAU

We had a very cold winter one year—a great deal of snow, which froze as it fell and lay a long time on the hard ground. We woke up one morning in a perfectly still white world. It had snowed heavily during the night, and the house was surrounded by a glistening white carpet which stretched away to the "sapinette" at the top of the lawn without a speck or flaw. There was no trace of path or road, or little low shrubs, and even the branches of the big lime-trees were heavy with snow. It was a bright, beautiful day—blue sky and a not too pale winter sun. Not a vehicle of any kind had ventured out. In the middle of the road were footprints deep in the snow where evidently the keepers and some workmen had passed. Nothing and no one had arrived from outside, neither postman, butcher, nor baker. The chef was in a wild state; but I assured him we could get on with eggs and game, of which there was always a provision for one day at any rate.

About eleven, Pauline and I started out. We thought we would go as far as the lodge and see what was going on on the highroad. We put on thick boots, gaiters and very short skirts, and had imagined we could walk in the footsteps of the keepers; but, of course, we couldn't take their long stride, and we floundered about in the snow. In some places where it had drifted we went in over our knees.

There was nothing visible on the road—not a creature, absolute stillness; a line of footprints in the middle where some labourer had passed, and the long stretch of white fields, broken by lines of black poplars running straight away to the forest.

While we were standing at the gate talking to old Antoine, who was all muffled up with a woollen comforter tied over his cap, and socks over his shoes, we saw a small moving object in the distance. As it came nearer we made out it was the postman, also so muffled up as to be hardly recognizable. He too had woollen socks over his shoes, and said the going was something awful, the "Montagne de Marolles" a sheet of ice; he had fallen twice, in spite of his socks and pointed stick. He said neither butcher nor baker would come—that no horse could get up the hill.

We sent him into the kitchen to thaw, and have his breakfast. That was one also of the traditions of the château; the postman always breakfasted. On Sundays, when there was no second delivery, he brought his little girl and an accordion, and remained all the afternoon. He often got a lift back to La Ferté, when the carriage was going in to the station, or the chef to market in the donkey-cart. *Now* many of the postmen have bicycles.

We had a curious feeling of being quite cut off from the outside world. The children, Francis and Alice, were having a fine time in the stable-yard, where the men had made them two snow figures—man and woman (giants)—and they were pelting them with snowballs and tumbling headlong into the heaps of snow on each side of the gate, where a passage had been cleared for the horses.

We thought it would be a good opportunity to do a little coasting and inaugurate a sled we had had made with great difficulty the year before. It was rather a long operation. The wheelwright at Marolles had never seen anything of the kind, had no idea *what* we wanted. Fortunately Francis had a little sled which one of his cousins had sent him from America; and with that as a model, and many explanations, the wheelwright and the blacksmith produced really a very creditable sled—quite large, a seat for two in front, and one behind for the person who steered. Only when the sled was finished the snow had disappeared! It rarely lasts long in France.

We had the sled brought out—the runners needed a little repairing—and the next day made our first attempt. There was not much danger of meeting anything. A sort of passage had been cleared, and gravel sprinkled in the middle of the road; but very few vehicles had passed, and the snow was as hard as ice. All the establishment "assisted" at the first trial, and the stable-boy accompanied us with the donkey who was to pull the sled up the hill.

We had some little difficulty in starting, Pauline and I in front, Francis behind; but as soon as we got fairly on the slope the thing flew. Pauline was frightened to death, screaming, and wanted to get off; but I held her tight, and we landed in the ditch near the foot of the hill. Half-way down (the hill is steep but straight, one sees a great distance) Francis saw the diligence arriving; and as he was not quite sure of his steering-gear, he thought it was better to take no risks, and steered us straight into the ditch as hard as we could go. The sled upset; we all rolled off into the deep soft snow, lost our hats, and emerged quite white from head to foot.

The diligence had stopped at the foot of the hill. There were only two men in it besides the driver, the old Père Jacques, who was dumbfounded when he recognized Madame Waddington. It seems they couldn't think what had happened. As they got to the foot of the hill, they saw a good many people at the gate of the château; then suddenly something detached itself from the group and rushed wildly down the hill. They thought it was an accident, some part of a carriage broken, and before they had time to collect their senses the whole thing collapsed in the ditch. The poor old man was quite disturbed—couldn't think we were not hurt, and begged us to get into the diligence and not trust ourselves again to such a dangerous vehicle. However we reassured him, and all walked up the hill together, the donkey pulling the sled, which was tied to him with a very primitive arrangement of ropes, the sled constantly swinging round and hitting him on the legs, which he naturally resented and kicked viciously.

We amused ourselves very much as long as the snow lasted, about ten days—coasted often, and made excursions to the neighbouring villages with the sled and the donkey. We wanted to skate, but that was not easy to arrange, as the ponds and "tourbières" near us were very deep, and I was afraid to venture with the children. I told Hubert, the coachman, who knew the country well, to see what he could find. He said there was a very good pond in the park of the château of La Ferté, and he was sure the proprietor, an old man who lived there by himself, would be quite pleased to let us come there.

The old gentleman was most amiable—begged we would come as often as we liked—merely making one condition, that we should have a man on the bank (the pond was only about a foot deep) with a rope in case of accidents.... We went there nearly every afternoon, and made quite a comfortable "installation" on the bank: a fire, rugs, chairs and a very good little goûter, the grocer's daughter bringing us hot wine and biscuits from the town.

It was a perfect sight for La Ferté. The whole town came to look at us, and the carters stopped their teams on the road to look on—one day particularly when one of our cousins, Maurice de Bunsen,[3] was staying with us. He skated beautifully, doing all sorts of figures, and his double eights and initials astounded the simple country folk. For some time after they spoke of "l'Anglais" who did such wonderful things on the ice.

They were bad days for the poor. We used to meet all the children coming back from school when we went home. The poor little things toiled up the steep, slippery hill, with often a cold wind that must have gone through the thin worn-out jackets and shawls they had for all covering, carrying their satchels and remnants of dinner. Those that came from a distance always brought their dinner with them, generally a good hunk of bread and a piece of chocolate, the poorer ones bread alone, very often only a stale hard crust that couldn't have been very nourishing. They were a very poor lot at our little village, St. Quentin, and we did all we could in the way of warm stockings and garments; but the pale, pinched faces rather haunted me, and Henrietta and I thought we would try and arrange with the school mistress who was wife of one of the keepers, to give them a hot plate of soup every day during the winter months. W., who knew his people well, rather discouraged us—said they all had a certain sort of pride, notwithstanding their poverty, and might perhaps be offended at being treated like tramps or beggars; but we could try if we liked.

We got a big kettle at La Ferté, and the good Mère Cécile of the Asile lent us the tin bowls, also telling us we wouldn't be able to carry out our plan. She had tried at the Asile, but it didn't go; the children didn't care about the soup—liked the bread and chocolate better. It was really a curious experience. I am still astonished when I think of it. The soup was made at the head-keeper's cottage, standing on the edge of the woods.

We went over the first day about eleven o'clock—a cold, clear day, a biting wind blowing down the valley. The children were all assembled, waiting impatiently for us to come. The soup was smoking in a big pot hung high over the fire. We, of course, tasted it, borrowing two bowls from the children and asking

[3] To-day British Embassador at Madrid.

Madame Labbey to cut us two pieces of bread, the children all giggling and rather shy. The soup was very good, and we were quite pleased to think that the poor little things should have something warm in their stomachs. The first depressing remark was made by our own coachman on the way home. His little daughter was living at the keeper's. I said to him, "I did not see Celine with the other children." "Oh, no, Madame; she wasn't there. We pay for the food at Labbey's; she doesn't need charity."

The next day, equally cold, about half the children came (there were only twenty-seven in the school); the third, five or six, rather shamefaced; the fourth, not one; and at the end of the week the keeper's wife begged us to stop the distribution; all the parents were hurt at the idea of their children receiving *public* charity from Madame Waddington. She had thought some of the very old people of the village might like what was left; but no one came except some tramps and rough-looking men who had heard there was food to be had, and they made her very nervous prowling around the house when she was alone, her husband away all day in the woods.

W. was amused—not at all surprised—said he was quite sure we shouldn't succeed, but it was just as well to make our own experience. We took our bowls back sadly to the Asile, where the good sister shook her head, saying, "Madame verra comme c'est difficile de faire du bien dans ce paysci; on ne pense qu'à s'amuser." And yet we saw the miserable little crusts of hard bread, and some of the boys in linen jackets over their skin, no shirt, and looking as if they had never had a good square meal in their lives.

I had one other curious experience, and after that I gave up trying anything that was a novelty or that they hadn't seen all their lives. The French peasant is really conservative; and if left to himself, with no cheap political papers or socialist orators haranguing in the cafes on the eternal topic of the rich and the poor, he would be quite content to go on leading the life he and his fathers have always led—would never want to destroy or change anything.

I was staying one year with Lady Derby at Knowsley, in Christmas week, and I was present one afternoon when she was making her annual distribution of clothes to the village children. I was much pleased with some ulsters and some red cloaks she had for the girls. They were so pleased, too—broad smiles on their faces when they were called up and the cloaks put on their shoulders. They looked so warm and comfortable, when the little band trudged home across the snow. I had instantly visions of my school children attired in these cloaks, climbing our steep hills in the dark winter days.

I had a long consultation with Lady Margaret Cecil, Lady Derby's daughter—a perfect saint, who spent all her life helping other people—and she gave me the catalogue of "Price Jones," a well-known Welsh shop whose "spécialité" was all sorts of clothes for country people, schools, workmen's families, etc. I ordered a large collection of red cloaks, ulsters, and flannel shirts at a very reasonable price, and they promised to send them in the late summer, so that we should find them when we went back to France.

We found two large cases when we got home, and were quite pleased at all the nice warm cloaks we had in store for the winter.

As soon as the first real cold days began, about the end of November, the women used to appear at the château asking for warm clothes for the children. The first one to come was the wife of the "garde de Borny"—a slight, pale woman, the mother of nine small children (several of them were members of the school at St. Quentin, who had declined our soup, and I rather had *their* little pinched, bloodless faces in my mind when I first thought about it). She had three with her—a baby in her arms, a boy and a girl of six and seven, both bare-legged, the boy in an old worn-out jersey pulled over his chest, the girl in a ragged blue and white apron, a knitted shawl over her head and shoulders. The baby had a cloak. I don't believe there was much on underneath, and the mother was literally a bundle of rags, her skirt so patched one could hardly make out the original colour, and a wonderful cloak all frayed at the ends and with holes in every direction. However, they were all clean.

The baby and the boy were soon provided for. The boy was much pleased with his flannel shirt. Then we produced the red cloak for the girl. The woman's face fell: "Oh, no, Madame, I couldn't take that; my little girl couldn't wear it." I, astounded: "But you don't see what it is—a good, thick cloak that will cover her all up and keep her warm." "Oh, no, Madame, she couldn't wear that; all the people on the road would laugh at her! Cela ne se porte pas dans notre pays" (that is not worn in our country).

I explained that I had several, and that she would see all the other little girls with the same cloaks; but I got only the same answer, adding that Madame would see—no child would wear such a cloak. I was much disgusted—thought the woman was capricious; but she was perfectly right; not a single mother, and Heaven knows they were poor enough, would take a red cloak, and they all had to be transformed into red flannel petticoats. Every woman made me the same answer: "Every one on the road would laugh at them."

I was not much luckier with the ulsters. What I had ordered for big girls of nine and ten would just go on girls of six and seven. Either French children are much stouter than English, or they wear thicker things underneath. Here again there was work to do—all the sleeves were much too long; my maids had to alter and shorten them, which they did with rather a bad grace.

A most interesting operation that very cold year was taking ice out of the big pond at the foot of the hill. The ice was several inches thick, and beautifully clear in the middle of the pond; toward the edges the reeds and long grass had all got frozen into it, and it was rather difficult to get the big blocks out. We had one of the farm carts with a pair of strong horses, and three or four men with axes and a long pointed stick. It was so solid that we all stood on the pond while the men were cutting their first square hole in the middle. It was funny to see the fish swimming about under the ice.

The whole village of course looked on, and the children were much excited, and wanted to come and slide on the ice, but I got nervous as the hole got bigger and the ice at the edges thinner, so we all adjourned to the road and watched operations from there.

There were plenty of fish in the pond, and once a year it was thoroughly drained and cleaned—the water drawn off, and the bottom of the pond, which got choked up with mud and weeds, cleared out. They made a fine haul of fish on those occasions from the small pools that were left on each side while the cleaning was going on.

Our ice-house was a godsend to all the countryside. Whenever any one was ill, and ice was wanted, they always came to the château. Our good old doctor was not at all in the movement as regarded fresh air and cold water, but ice he often wanted. He was a rough, kindly old man, quite the type of the country practitioner—a type that is also disappearing, like everything else. Everybody knew his cabriolet (with a box at the back where he kept his medicine chest and instruments), with a strong brown horse that trotted all day and all night up and down the steep hills in all weathers. A very small boy was always with him to hold the horse while he made his visits.

Our doctor was very kind to the poor, and never refused to go out at night. It was funny to see him arrive on a cold day, enveloped in so many cloaks and woollen comforters that it took him some time to get out of his wraps. He had a gruff voice, and heavy black overhanging eyebrows which frightened people at first, but they soon found out what a kind heart there was beneath such a rough exterior, and the children loved him. He had always a box of liquorice lozenges in his waistcoat pocket which he distributed freely to the small ones.

The country doctors about us now are a very different type—much younger men, many foreigners. There are two Russians and a Greek in some of the small villages near us. I believe they are very good. I met the Greek one day at the keeper's cottage. He was looking after the keeper's wife, who was very ill. It seemed funny to see a Greek, with one of those long Greek names ending in "popolo," in a poor little French village almost lost in the woods; but he made a very good impression on me—was very quiet, didn't give too much medicine (apothecaries' bills are always such a terror to the poor), and spoke kindly to the woman. He comes still in a cabriolet, but his Russian colleague has an automobile—indeed so have now many of the young French doctors. I think there is a little rivalry between the Frenchmen and the foreigners, but the latter certainly make their way.

What is very serious now is the open warfare between the curé and the school-master. When I first married, the school-masters and mistresses took their children to church, always sat with them and kept them in order. The school-mistress sometimes played the organ. Now they not only don't go to church themselves, but they try to prevent the children from going. The result is that half the children don't go either to the church or to the catechism.

I had a really annoying instance of this state of things one year when we wanted to make a Christmas tree and distribution of warm clothes at Montigny, a lonely little village not far from us. We talked it over with the curé and the school-master. They gave us the names and ages of all the children, and were both much pleased to have a fête in their quiet little corner. I didn't suggest a service in the church, as I thought that might perhaps be a difficulty for the school-master.

Two days before the fête I had a visit from the curé of Montigny, who looked embarrassed and awkward; had evidently something on his mind, and finally blurted out that he was very sorry he couldn't be present at the Christmas tree, as he was obliged to go to Reims that day. I, much surprised and decidedly put out: "You are going to Reims the one day in the year when we come and make a fête in your village? It is most extraordinary, and surprises me extremely. The date has been fixed for weeks, and I hold very much to your being there."

He still persisted, looking very miserable and uncomfortable, and finally said he was going away on purpose, so as not to be at the school-house. He liked the school-master very much, got on with him perfectly; he was intelligent and taught the children very well; but all school-masters who had anything to do with the Church or the curé were "malnotés." The mayor of Montigny was a violent radical; and surely if he heard that the curé was present at our fête in the school-house, the school-master would be dismissed the next day. The man was over thirty, with wife and children; it would be difficult for him to find any other employment; and he himself would regret him, as his successor might be much worse and fill the children's heads with impossible ideas.

I was really very much vexed, and told him I would talk it over with my son and see what we could do. The poor little curé was much disappointed, but begged me not to insist upon his presence.

A little later the school-master arrived, also very much embarrassed, saying practically the same thing—that he liked the curé very much. He never talked politics, nor interfered in any way with his parishioners. Whenever any one was ill or in trouble, he was always the first person to come forward and nurse and help. But he saw him very little. If I held to the curé being present at the Christmas tree, of course he could say nothing; but he would certainly be dismissed the next day. He was married—had nothing but his salary; it would be a terrible blow to him.

I was very much perplexed, particularly as the time was short and I couldn't get hold of the mayor. So we called a family council—Henrietta and Francis were both at home—and decided that we must let our fête take place without the curé. The school-master was very grateful, and said he would take my letter to the post-office. I had to write to the curé to tell him what we had decided, and that he might go to Reims.

One of our great amusements in the winter was the hunting. We knew very well the two gentlemen, Comtes de B. and de L., who hunted the Villers-Cotterets forest, and often rode with them. It was beautiful riding country—stretches of grass alongside the hard highroad, where one could have a capital canter, the only difficulty being the quantity of broad, low ditches made for the water to run off. Once the horses knew them they took them quite easily in their stride, but they were a little awkward to manage at first. The riding was very different from the Roman Campagna, which was my only experience. There was very little to jump; long straight alleys, with sometimes a big tree across the road, occasionally ditches; nothing like the very stiff fences and stone walls one meets in the Campagna, or the slippery bits of earth (tufa) where the horses used to slide sometimes in the most uncomfortable way. One could gallop for miles in the Villers-Cotterets forest with a loose rein. It was disagreeable sometimes when we left the broad alleys and took little paths in and out of the trees. When the wood was thick and the branches low, I was always afraid one would knock me off the saddle or come into my eyes. Some of the meets were most picturesque; sometimes in the heart of the forest at a great carrefour, alleys stretching off in every direction, hemmed in by long straight lines of winter trees on each side, with a thick, high undergrowth of ferns, and a broad-leaved plant I didn't know, which remained green almost all winter. It was pretty to see the people arriving from all sides, in every description of vehicle—breaks, dog-carts, victorias, farmer's gigs—grooms with led horses, hunting men in green or red coats, making warm bits of colour in the rather severe landscape. The pack of hounds, white with brown spots, big, powerful animals, gave the valets de chiens plenty to do. Apparently they knew all their names, as we heard frequent admonitions to Comtesse, Diane (a very favourite name for hunting dogs in France), La Grise, etc., to keep quiet, and not make little excursions into the woods. As the words were usually accompanied by a cut of the whip, the dogs understood quite well, and remained a compact mass on the side of the road. There was the usual following of boys, tramps, and stray bûcherons (woodmen), and when the day was fine, and the meet not too far, a few people would come from the neighbouring villages, or one or two carriages from the livery stables of Villers-Cotterets, filled with strangers who had been attracted by the show and the prospect of spending an afternoon in the forest. A favourite meet was at the pretty little village of Ivors, standing just on the edge of the forest not far from us. It consisted of one long street, a church, and a château at one end. The château had been a fine one, but was fast going to ruin, uninhabited, paint and plaster falling off, roof and walls remaining, and showing splendid proportions, but had an air of decay and neglect that was sad to see in such a fine place. The owner never lived there; had several other places. An agent came down occasionally, and looked after the farm and woods. There was a fine double court-yard and enormous "communs," a large field only separating the kitchen garden from the forest. A high wall in fairly good condition surrounded the garden and small park. On a hunting morning the little place quite waked up, and it was pretty to see the dogs and horses grouped under the walls of the old château, and the hunting men in their bright coats moving about among the peasants and carters in their dark-blue smocks.

The start was very pretty—one rode straight into the forest, the riders spreading in all directions. The field was never very large—about thirty—I the only lady. The cor de chasse was a delightful novelty to me, and I soon learned all the calls—the débouché, the vue and the hallali, when the poor beast is at the last gasp. The first time I saw the stag taken I was quite miserable. We had had a splendid gallop. I was piloted by one of the old stagers, who knew every inch of the forest, and who promised I should be in at the death, if I would follow him, "mais il faut me suivre partout, avez-vous peur?" As he was very stout, and not particularly well mounted, and I had a capital English mare, I was quite sure I could pass wherever he could. He took me through all sorts of queer little paths, the branches sometimes so low that it didn't seem possible to get through, but we managed it. Sometimes we lost sight of the hunt entirely, but he always guided himself by the sound of the horns, which one hears at a great distance. Once a stag bounded across the road just in front of us, making our horses shy violently, but he said that was not the one we were after. I wondered how he knew, but didn't ask any questions. Once or twice we stopped in the thick of the woods, having apparently lost ourselves entirely, not hearing a sound, and then in the distance there would be the faint sound of the horn, enough for him to distinguish the vue, which meant that they were still running. Suddenly, very near, we heard the great burst of the hallali—horses, dogs, riders, all joining in; and pushing through the brushwood we found ourselves on the edge of a big pond, almost a lake. The stag, a fine one, was swimming about, nearly finished, his eyes starting out of his head, and his breast shaken with great sobs. The whole pack of dogs was swimming after him, the hunters all swarming down to the edge, sounding their horns, and the master of hounds following in a small flatboat, waiting to give the coup de grâce with his carbine when the poor beast should attempt to get up the bank. It was a sickening sight. I couldn't stand it, and retreated (we had all dismounted) back into the woods, much to the surprise and disgust of my companion, who was very proud and pleased at having brought me in at the death among the very first. Of course, one gets hardened, and a stag at bay is a fine sight. In the forest they usually make their last stand against a big tree, and sell their lives dearly. The dogs sometimes get an ugly blow. I was really very glad always when the stag got away. I had all the pleasure and excitement of the hunt without having my feelings lacerated at the end of the day. The sound of the horns and the unwonted stir in the country had brought out all the neighbourhood, and the inhabitants of the little village, including the curé and the châtelaine of the small château near, soon appeared upon the scene. The curé, a nice, kindly faced old man, with white hair and florid complexion, was much interested in all the details of the hunt. It seems the stag is often taken in these ponds, les étangs de la ramée, which are quite a feature in the country, and one of the sights of the Villers-Cotterets forest, where strangers are always brought. They are very picturesque; the trees slope down to the edge of the ponds, and when the bright autumn foliage is reflected in the water the effect is quite charming.

Mme. de M., the châtelaine, was the type of the grande dame Française, fine, clear-cut features, black eyes, and perfectly white hair, very well arranged. She was no longer young, but walked with a quick, light step, a cane in her hand. She, too, was much interested, such an influx of people, horses, dogs, and carriages (for in some mysterious way the various vehicles always seemed to find their way to the finish). It was an event in the quiet little village. She admired my mare very much, which instantly won my affections. She asked us to come back with her to the château—it was only about a quarter of an hour's walk—to have some refreshment after our long day; so I held up my skirt as well as I could, and we walked along together. The château is not very large, standing close to the road in a small park, really more of a manor house than a château. She took us into the drawing-room just as stiff and bare as all the others I had seen, a polished parquet floor, straight-backed, hard chairs against the wall (the old lady herself looked as if she had sat up straight on a hard chair all her life). In the middle of the room was an enormous palm-tree going straight up to the ceiling. She said it had been there for years and always remained when she went to Paris in the spring. She was a widow, lived alone in the château with the old servants. Her daughter and grandchildren came occasionally to stay with her. She gave us wine and cake, and was most agreeable. I saw her often afterward, both in the country and Paris, and loved to hear her talk. She had remained absolutely ancien régime, couldn't understand modern life and ways at all. One of the things that shocked her beyond words was to see her granddaughters and their young friends playing tennis with young men in flannels. In her day a young man in bras de chemise would have been ashamed to appear before ladies in such attire. We didn't stay very long that day, as we were far from home, and the afternoon was shortening fast. The retraite was sometimes long when we had miles of hard road before us, until we arrived at the farm or village where the carriage was waiting. When we could walk our horses it was bearable, but sometimes when they broke into a jog-trot, which nothing apparently could make them change, it was very fatiguing after a long day.

Sometimes, when we had people staying with us, we followed the hunt in the carriage. We put one of the keepers of the Villers-Cotterets forest on the box, and it was wonderful how much we could see. The meet was always amusing, but when once the hunt had moved off, and the last stragglers disappeared in the forest, it didn't seem as if there was any possibility of catching them; and sometimes we would drive in a perfectly opposite direction, but the old keeper knew all about the stags and their haunts when they would break out and cross the road, and when they would double and go back into the woods. We were waiting one day in the heart of the forest, at one of the carrefours, miles away apparently from everything, and an absolute stillness around us. Suddenly there came a rush and noise of galloping horses, baying hounds and horns, and a flash of red and green coats dashed by, disappearing in an instant in the thick woods before we had time to realize what it was. It was over in a moment—seemed an hallucination. We saw and heard nothing more, and the same intense stillness surrounded us. We had the same sight, the stag taken in the water, some years later, when we were alone at the château. Mme. A. was dead, and her husband had gone to Paris to live. We were sitting in the gallery one day after breakfast, finishing our coffee, and making plans for the day, when suddenly we saw red spots and moving figures in the distance, on the hills opposite, across the canal. Before we had time to get glasses and see what was happening, the children came rushing in to say the hunt was in the woods opposite, the horns sounding the hallali, and the stag probably in the canal. With the glasses we made out the riders quite distinctly, and soon heard faint echoes of the horn. We all made a rush for hats and coats, and started off to the canal. We had to go down a steep, slippery path which was always muddy in all weathers, and across a rather rickety narrow plank, also very slippery. As we got nearer, we heard the horns very well, and the dogs yelping. By the time we got to the bridge, which was open to let a barge go through, everything had disappeared—horses, dogs, followers, and not a sound of horn or hoof. One solitary horseman only, who had evidently lost the hunt and didn't know which way to go. We lingered a little, much disgusted, but still hoping we might see something, when suddenly we heard again distant sounds of horns and yelping dogs. The man on the other side waved his cap wildly, pointed to the woods, and started off full gallop. In a few minutes the hill slope was alive with hunters coming up from all sides. We were nearly mad with impatience, but couldn't swim across the canal, the bridge was still open, the barge lumbering through. The children with their Fräulein and some of the party crossed a little lower down on a crazy little plank, which I certainly shouldn't have dared attempt, and at last the bargeman took pity on us and put us across. We raced along the bank as fast as we could, but the canal turns a great deal, and a bend prevented our seeing the stag, with the hounds at his heels, galloping down the slope and finally jumping into the canal, just where it widens out and makes a sort of lake between our hamlet of Bourneville and Marolles. It was a pretty sight, all the hunters dismounted, walking along the edge of the water, sounding their hallali, the entire population of Bourneville and Marolles and all our household arriving in hot haste, and groups of led horses and valets de chiens in their green coats half-way up the slope. The stag, a very fine one, was swimming round and round, every now and then making an effort to get up the bank, and falling back heavily—he was nearly done, half his body sinking in the water, and his great eyes looking around to see if any one would help him. I went back to the barge (they had stayed, too, to see the sight), and the woman, a nice, clean, motherly body with two babies clinging to her, was much excited over the cruelty of the thing.

"Madame trouve que c'est bien de tourmenter une pauvre bête qui ne fait de mal à personne, pour s'amuser?" Madame found that rather difficult to answer, and turned the conversation to her life on the barge. The minute little cabin looked clean, with several pots of red geraniums, clean muslin curtains, a canary bird, and a nondescript sort of dog, who, she told me, was very useful, taking care of the children and keeping them from falling into the water when she was obliged to leave them on the boat while she went on shore to get her provisions. I asked: "*How* does he keep them from falling into the water—does he take hold of their clothes?" "No, I leave them in the cabin, when I am obliged to go ashore, and he stands at the door and barks and won't let them come out." While I was talking to her I heard a shot, and realised that the poor stag had been finished at last. It was early in the afternoon—three o'clock, and I suggested that the whole chasse should adjourn to the château for goûter. This they promptly accepted, and started off to find their horses. Then I had some misgivings as to what I could give them for goûter. We were a small party, mostly women and children. W. was away, and I thought that probably the chef, who was a sportsman as well as a cook, was shooting (he had hired a small chasse not far from us); I had told him there was nothing until dinner. I had visions of twenty or thirty hungry men and an ordinary tea-table, with some thin bread and butter, a pot of damson jam, and some sables, so I sent off Francis's tutor, the stable-boy, and the gardener's boy to the château as fast as their legs could carry them, to find somebody, anybody, to prepare us as much food as they could, and to sacrifice the dinner at once, to make sandwiches—tea and chocolate, of course, were easily provided.

I suggested that the whole chasse should adjourn to the château.

We all started back to the house up the steep, muddy path, some of the men with us leading their horses, some riding round by Marolles to give orders to the breaks and various carriages to come to the château. The big gates were open, Hubert there to arrange at once for the accommodation of so many horses and equipages, and the billiard and dining-rooms, with great wood-fires, looking most comfortable. The chasseurs begged not to come into the drawing-room, as they were covered with mud, so they brushed off what they could in the hall, and we went at once to the goûter. It was funny to see our quiet dining-room invaded by such a crowd of men, some red-coated, some green, all with breeches and high muddy boots. The master of hounds, M. Menier, proposed to make the curée on the lawn after tea, which I was delighted to accept. We had an English cousin staying with us who knew all about hunting in her own country, but had never seen a French chasse à courre, and she was most keen about it. The goûter was very creditable. It seems that they had just caught the chef, who had been attracted by the unusual sounds and bustle on the hillside, and who had also come down to see the show. He promptly grasped the situation, hurried back to the house, and produced beef and mayonnaise sandwiches, and a splendid savarin with whipped cream in the middle (so we naturally didn't have any dessert—but nobody minded), tea, chocolate, and whiskey, of course. As soon as it began to get dark we all adjourned to the lawn. All the carriages, the big breaks with four horses, various lighter vehicles, grooms and led horses were massed at the top of the lawn, just where it rises slightly to meet the woods. A little lower down was Hubert, the huntsman (a cousin of our coachman, Hubert, who was very pleased to do the honours of his stable-yard), with one or two valets de chiens, the pack of dogs, and a great whip, which was very necessary to keep the pack back until he allowed them to spring upon the carcass of the stag. He managed them beautifully. Two men held up the stag—the head had already been taken off; it was a fine one, with broad, high antlers, a dix cors. Twice Hubert led his pack up, all yelping and their eyes starting out of their heads, and twice drove them back, but the third time he let them spring on the carcass. It was an ugly sight, the compact mass of dogs, all snarling and struggling, noses down and tails up. In a few minutes nothing was left of the poor beast but bones, and not many of them. Violet had les honneurs du pied (the hoof of one of the hind legs of the stag), which is equivalent to the "brush" one gives in fox-hunting. She thanked M. M., the master of hounds, very prettily and said she would have it arranged and hang it up in the hall of her English home, in remembrance of a lovely winter afternoon, and her first experience of what still remains of the old French vénerie. The horns sounded again the curée and the depart, and the whole company gradually dispersed, making quite a cortège as they moved down the avenue, horses and riders disappearing in the gray mist that was creeping up from the canal, and the noise of wheels and hoofs dying away in the distance.

Some red-coated, some green, all with breeches and high muddy boots.

We were pottering about in our woods one day, waiting for Labbez (the keeper) to come and decide about some trees that must be cut down, when a most miserable group emerged from one of the side alleys and slipped by so quickly and quietly that we couldn't speak to them. A woman past middle age, lame, unclothed really—neither shoes nor stockings, not even a chemise—two sacks of coarse stuff, one tied around her waist half covering her bare legs, one over her shoulders; two children with her, a big overgrown girl of about twelve, equally without clothing, an old black bodice gaping open over her bare skin, held together by one button, a short skirt so dirty and torn that one wondered what kept it on, no shoes nor stockings, black hair falling straight down over her forehead and eyes; the boy, about six, in a dirty apron, also over his bare skin. I was horrified, tried to make them turn and speak to me, but they disappeared under the brushwood as quickly as they could, "evidently up to no good," said W. In a few moments the keeper appeared, red and breathless, having been running after poachers—a woman the worst of the lot. We described the party we had just seen, and he was wildly excited, wanted to start again in pursuit, said they were just the ones he was looking for. The woman belonged to a band of poachers and vagabonds they could not get hold of. They could trace her progress sometimes by the blood on the grass where the thorns and sharp stones had torn her feet. It seems they were quite a band, living anywhere in the woods, in old charcoal-burners' huts or under the trees, never staying two nights in the same place. There are women, and children, and babies, who appear and disappear, in the most extraordinary manner. Many of them have been condemned, and have had two weeks or a month of prison. One family is employed by one of the small farmers near, who lets them live in a tumbledown hut in the midst of his woods, and that is their centre. We passed by there two or three days later, when we were riding across the fields, and anything so miserable I never saw; the house half falling to pieces, no panes of glass, dirty rags stuffed in the windows, no door at all, bundles of dirty straw inside, a pond of filthy water at one side of the house, two or three dirty children playing in it, and inside at the opening, where the door should have been, the same lame woman in her two sacks. She glowered at us, standing defiantly at the opening to prevent our going in, in case we had any such intention. I suppose she had various rabbits and hares hung up inside she couldn't have accounted for. There was no other habitation anywhere near; no cart or vehicle of any kind could have got there. We followed a narrow path, hardly visible in the long grass, and the horses had to pick their way—one couldn't imagine a more convenient trysting-place for vagabonds and tramps. It seems incredible that such things should go on at our doors, so to speak, but it is very difficult to get at them. Our keepers and M. de M., whose property touches ours, have had various members of the gang arrested, but they always begin again. The promiscuity of living is something awful, girls and young men squatting and sleeping in the same room on heaps of dirty rags. There have been some arrests for infanticide, when a baby's appearance and disappearance was too flagrant, but the girls don't care. They do their time of prison, come out quite untamed by prison discipline, and begin again their wild, free life. One doesn't quite understand the farmer who gives any shelter to such a bad lot, but I fancy there is a tacit understanding that his hares and rabbits must be left unmolested.

It is amusing to see the keepers when they suspect poachers are in their woods. When the leaves are off they can see at a great distance, and with their keen, trained eyes make out quite well when a moving object is a hare, or a roe-buck, or a person on all fours, creeping stealthily along. They have powerful glasses, too, which help them very much. They, too, have their various tricks, like the poachers. As the gun-barrel is seen at a great distance when the sun strikes it, they cover it with a green stuff that takes the general tint of the leaves and the woods, and post themselves, half hidden in the bushes, near some of the quarries, where the poachers generally come. Then they give a gun to an under-strapper, telling him to stand in some prominent part of the woods, *his* gun well in sight. That, of course, the poachers see at once, so they make straight for the other side, and often fall upon the keepers who are lying in wait for them. As a general rule, they don't make much resistance, as they know the keepers will shoot—not to kill them, but a shot in the ankle or leg that will disable them for some time. I had rather a weakness for one poaching family. The man was young, good-looking, and I don't really believe a bad lot, but he had been unfortunate, had naturally a high temper, and couldn't stand being howled at and sworn at when things didn't go exactly as the patron wanted; consequently he never stayed in any place, tried to get some other work, but was only fit for the woods, where he knew every tree and root and the habits and haunts of all the animals. He had a pretty young wife and two children, who had also lived in the woods all their lives, and could do nothing else. The wife came to see me one day to ask for some clothes for herself and the children, which I gave, of course, and then tried mildly to speak to her about her husband, who spent half his time in prison, and was so sullen and scowling when he came out that everybody gave him a wide berth. The poor thing burst into a passion of tears and incoherent defence of her husband. Everybody had been so hard with him. When he had done his best, been up all night looking after the game, and then was rated and sworn at by his master before every one because un des Parisiens didn't know what to do with a gun when he had one in his hand, and couldn't shoot a hare that came and sat down in front of him, it was impossible not to answer un peu vivement peut-être, and it was hard to be discharged at once without a chance of finding anything else, etc., and at last winding up with the admission that he did take hares and rabbits occasionally; but when there was nothing to eat in the house and the children were crying with hunger, what was he to do? Madame would never have known or missed the rabbits, and after all, le Bon Dieu made them for everybody. I tried to persuade W. to take him as a workman in the woods, with the hope of getting back as under-keeper, but he would not hear of it, said the man was perfectly unruly and violent-tempered, and would demoralize all the rest. They remained some time in the country, and the woman came sometimes to see me, but she had grown hard, evidently thought I could have done something for her husband, and couldn't understand that as long as he went on snaring game no one would have anything to do with him—always repeating the same thing, that a Bon Dieu had made the animals pour tout le monde. Of course it must be an awful temptation for a man who has starving children at home, and who knows that he has only to walk a few yards in the woods to find rabbits in plenty; and one can understand the feeling that le Bon Dieu provided food for all his children, and didn't mean some to starve, while others lived on the fat of the land.

It was a long time before I could get accustomed to seeing women work in the fields (which I had never seen in America). In the cold autumn days, when they were picking the betterave (a big beet root) that is used to make sugar in France, it made me quite miserable to see them. Bending all day over the long rows of beets, which required quite an effort to pull out of the hard earth, their hands red and chapped, sometimes a cold wind whistling over the fields that no warm garment could keep out, and they never had any really warm garment. We met an old woman one day quite far from any habitation, who was toiling home, dragging her feet, in wretched, half-worn shoes, over the muddy country roads, who stopped and asked us if we hadn't a warm petticoat to give her. She knew me, called me by name, and said she lived in the little hamlet near the château. She looked miserably cold and tired. I asked where she came from, and what she had been doing all day. "Scaring the crows in M. A.'s fields," was the answer. "What does your work consist of?" I asked. "Oh, I just sit there and make a noise—beat the top of an old tin kettle with sticks and shake a bit of red stuff in the air." Poor old woman, she looked half paralyzed with cold and fatigue, and I was really almost ashamed to be seated so warmly and comfortably in the carriage, well wrapped up in furs and rugs, and should have quite understood if she had poured out a torrent of abuse. It must rouse such bitter and angry feeling when these poor creatures, half frozen and half starved, see carriages rolling past with every appliance of wealth and luxury. I suppose what saves us is that they are so accustomed to their lives, the long days of hard work, the wretched, sordid homes, the insufficient meals, the quantities of children clamouring for food and warmth. Their parents and grandparents have lived the same lives, and anything else would seem as unattainable as the moon, or some fairy tale. There has been one enormous change in all the little cottages—the petroleum lamp. All have got one—petroleum is cheap and gives much more light and heat than the old-fashioned oil lamp. In the long winter afternoons, when one must have light for work of any kind, the petroleum lamp is a godsend. We often noticed the difference coming home late. The smallest hamlets looked quite cheerful with the bright lights shining through the cracks and windows. I can't speak much from *personal* experience of the *inside* of the cottages—I was never much given to visiting among the poor. I suppose I did not take it in the right spirit, but I could never see the poetry, the beautiful, patient lives, the resignation to their humble lot. I only saw the dirt, and smelt all the bad smells, and heard how bad most of the young ones were to all the poor old people. "Cela mange comme quatre, et cela n'est plus bon à rien," I heard one woman remark casually to her poor old father sitting huddled up in a heap near the fire. I don't know, either, whether they liked to have us come. What suited them best was to send the children to the château. They always got a meal and a warm jacket and petticoat.

Peasant women.

V

CEREMONIES AND FESTIVALS

We were very particular about attending all important ceremonies at La Ferté, as we rarely went to church there except on great occasions. We had our service regularly at the château every Sunday morning. All the servants, except ours, were Protestants, Swiss generally, and very respectable they looked—all the women in black dresses and white caps—when they assembled in M. A.'s library, sitting on cane chairs near the door.

Some, in fact most, Protestants in France attach enormous importance to having all their household Protestant. A friend of mine, a Protestant, having tea with me one day in Paris was rather pleased with the bread or little "croissants," and asked me where they came from. I said I didn't know, but would ask the butler. That rather surprised her. Then she said, "Your baker of course is a Protestant." That I didn't know either, and, what was much worse in her eyes, I didn't care. She was quite distressed, gave me the address of an excellent Swiss Protestant baker and begged me to sever all connection with the Catholic at once. I asked her if she really thought dangerous papist ideas were kneaded in with the bread, but she would not listen to my mild "persiflage," and went away rather anxious about my spiritual welfare.

We went always to the church at La Ferté for the fête of St. Cécile, as the Fanfare played in the church on that day. The Fanfare was a very important body. Nearly all the prominent citizens of La Ferté, who had any idea of music, were members—the butcher, the baker, the coiffeur, etc. The Mayor was president and walked at the head of the procession when they filed into the church. I was "Présidente d'Honneur" and always wore my badge pinned conspicuously on my coat. It was a great day for the little town. Weeks before the fête we used to hear all about it from the coiffeur when he came to the château to shave the gentlemen. He played the big drum and thought the success of the whole thing depended on his performance. He proposed to bring his instrument one morning and play his part for us. We were very careful to be well dressed on that day and discarded the short serge skirts we generally wore. All the La Ferté ladies, particularly the wives and sisters of the performers, put on their best clothes, and their feelings would have been hurt if we had not done the same.

In fact it was a little difficult to dress up to the occasion. The older women all had jet and lace on their dresses, with long trailing skirts, and the younger ones, even children, had wonderful hats with feathers—one or two long white ones.

It was a pretty, animated sight as we arrived. All along the road we had met bands of people hurrying on to the town—the children with clean faces and pinafores, the men with white shirts, and even the old grandmothers—their shawls on their shoulders and their turbans starched stiff—were hobbling along with their sticks, anxious to arrive. We heard sounds of music as we got to the church—the procession was evidently approaching. The big doors were wide open, a great many people already inside. We looked straight down the nave to the far end where the high altar, all flowers and candles, made a bright spot of colour. Red draperies and banners were hanging from the columns—vases and wreaths of flowers at the foot of the statues of the saints; chairs and music-stands in the chancel. We went at once to our places. The curé, with his choir boys in their little short white soutanes, red petticoats and red shoes, was just coming out of the sacristy and the procession was appearing at the bottom of the church. First came the Mayor in a dress coat and white cravat—the "Adjoint" and one of the municipal council just behind, then the banner—rather a heavy one, four men carried it. After that the "pompiers," all in uniform, each man carrying his instrument; they didn't play as they came up the aisle, stopped their music at the door; but when they did begin—I don't know exactly at what moment of the mass—it was something appalling. The first piece was a military march, executed with all the artistic conviction and patriotic ardour of their young lungs (they were mostly young men). We were at the top of the church, very near the performers, and the first bursts of trumpets and bugles made one jump. They played several times. It didn't sound too badly at the "Elevation" when they had chosen rather a soft (comparatively) simple melody. The curé preached a very pretty, short sermon, telling them about Saint Cécile, the delicately nurtured young Roman who was not afraid to face martyrdom and death for the sake of her religion. The men listened most attentively and seemed much interested when he told them how he had seen in Rome the church of St. Cécile built over the ruin of the saint's house—the sacristy just over her bath-room. I asked him how he could reconcile it to his conscience to speak of the *melodious* sounds that accompanied the prayers of the faithful, but he said one must look sometimes at the intention more than at the result.

There was a certain *harmony* among the men when they were practising and preparing their music for the church, and as long as they held to coming and gave up their evenings to practising, instead of spending them in the wine shops, we must do all we could to encourage them.

The procession went out in the same order—halted at the church door and then W. made them a nice little speech, saying he was pleased to see how numerous they were and how much improved—they would certainly take an honourable place in the concours de fanfares of the department. They escorted the Mayor back to his house playing their march and wound up with a copious déjeuner at the "Sauvage." Either the Mayor or the "Adjoint" always went to the banquet. W. gave the champagne, but abstained from the feast.

They really did improve as they went on. They were able to get better instruments and were stimulated by rival fanfares in the neighbourhood. They were very anxious to come and play at the château, and we promised they should whenever a fitting occasion should present itself.

We had a visit from the Staals one year. The Baron de Staal was Russian Ambassador in England, and we had been colleagues there for many years. We asked the Fanfare to come one Sunday afternoon while they were there. We had a little difficulty over the Russian National Hymn, which they, naturally, wanted to play. The Chef de Fanfare came to see me one day and we looked over the music together. I had it only for the piano, but I explained the tempo and repetitions to him and he arranged it very well for his men. They made quite an imposing entrance. Half the population of La Ferté escorted them (all much excited by the idea of seeing the Russian Ambassador), and they were reinforced by the two villages they passed through. We waited for them in the gallery—doors and windows open. They played the spirited French march "Sambre et Meuse" as they came up the avenue. It sounded quite fine in the open air. They halted and saluted quite in military style as soon as they came in front of the gallery—stopped their march and began immediately the Russian Hymn, playing it very well.

They were much applauded, we in the gallery giving the signal and their friends on the lawn joining in enthusiastically. They were a motley crowd—over a hundred I should think—ranging from the municipal councillor of La Ferté, in his high hat and black cloth Sunday coat, to the humpbacked daughter of the village carpenter and the idiot boy who lived in a cave on the road and frightened the children out of their wits by running out and making faces at them whenever they passed. They played three or four times, then W. called up one or two of the principal performers and presented them to the Staals. Mme. de Staal spoke to them very prettily, thanked them for playing the Russian Hymn and said she would like to hear the "Sambre et Meuse" again. That, of course, delighted them and they marched off to the strains of their favourite tune. About half-way down the avenue we heard a few cries of "Vive la Russie," and then came a burst of cheers.

Our dinner was rather pleasant that evening. We had the Préfet, M. Sebline; Senator of the Aisne, Jusserand, present Ambassador to Washington; Mme. Thénard, of the Comédie Française, and several young people. Jusserand is always a brilliant talker—so easy—no pose of any kind, and Sebline was interesting, telling about all sorts of old customs in the country.

Though we were so near Paris, hardly two hours by the express, the people had remained extraordinarily primitive. There were no manufacturing towns anywhere near us, nothing but big farms, forests and small far-apart villages. The modern socialist-radical ideas were penetrating very slowly into the heads of the people—they were quite content to be humble tillers of the soil, as their fathers had been before them. The men had worked all their lives on the farms, the women, too; beginning quite young, taking care of cows and geese, picking beet-root, etc.

What absolutely changed the men was the three years' military service. After knocking about in garrison towns, living with a great many people always, having all sorts of amusements easily at hand and a certain independence, once the service of the day was over, they found the dull regular routine of the farm very irksome. In the summer it was well enough—harvest-time was gay, everyone in the fields, but in the short, cold winter days, with the frozen ground making all the work doubly hard, just enough food and no distraction of any kind but a pipe in the kitchen after supper, the young men grew terribly restive and discontented. Very few of them remain, and the old traditions of big farms handed down from father to son for three or four generations are rapidly disappearing. After dinner we had music and some charming recitations by Mme. Thénard. Her first one was a comic monologue which always had the wildest success in London, "Je suis veuve," beginning it with a ringing peal of laughter which was curiously contagious—everyone in the room joined in. I like her better in some of her serious things. When she said "le bon gite" and "le petit clairon," by Paul Déroulède, in her beautiful deep voice, I had a decided choke in my throat.

We often had music at the château. Many of our artist friends came down—glad to have two or three days rest in the quiet old house. We had an amusing experience once with the young organist from La Ferté—almost turned his hair gray. He had taught himself entirely and managed his old organ very well. He had heard vaguely of Wagner and we had always promised him we would try and play some of his music with two pianos—eight hands. Four hands are really not enough for such complicated music. Mlle. Dubois, premier prix du conservatoire—a beautiful musician—was staying with us one year and we arranged a concert for one evening, asking the organist to come to dinner. The poor man was rather terrified at dining at the château—had evidently taken great pains with his dress (a bright pink satin cravat was rather striking) and thanked the butler most gratefully every time he handed him a dish—"Je vous remercie beaucoup, Monsieur." We had our two grand pianos and were going to play the overture of Tannhäuser, one of the simplest and most melodious of Wagner's compositions. The performers were Francis and I, Mlle. Dubois and the organist. It was a little difficult to arrange who he should play with. He was very nervous at the idea of playing with Mlle. Dubois—rather frightened of me and in absolute terror at the idea of playing before W. Finally it was decided that he and I should take the second piano—he playing the bass. It was really funny to see him; his eyes were fixed on the music and he counted audibly and breathlessly all the time, and I heard him muttering occasionally to himself, "Non ce n'est pas possible," "Non ce n'est pas cela."

I must say that the Walpurgis Night for a person playing at sight and unaccustomed to Wagner's music is an ordeal—however, he acquitted himself extremely well and we got through our performance triumphantly, but great drops of perspiration were on his forehead. W. was very nice to him and Mlle. Dubois quite charming, encouraging him very much. Still I don't think his evening at the château was one of unmixed pleasure, and I am sure he was glad to have that overture behind him.

We saw our neighbours very rarely; occasionally some men came to breakfast. The sous-préfet, one or two of the big farmers or some local swells who wanted to talk politics to W. One frequent visitor was an architect from Château-Thierry, who had built W.'s farm. He was an enormous man, very stout and red, always attired in shiny black broadcloth. He was a very shrewd specimen, very well up in all that went on in the country and very useful to W. He had a fine appetite, always tucking his napkin carefully under his chin when he sat down to table. He talked a great deal one day about his son, who had a good tenor voice and had just got an engagement at the Opéra Comique. Said he would like us to hear him sing—might he bring him some day to breakfast?

He came back two or three weeks later with the young man, who was a great improvement upon his father. The Paris boulevards and the coulisses of the opera had quite modified the young provincial. He talked a good deal at table, was naturally much pleased to have got into the Opéra Comique. As it is a "théâtre subventionné" (government theatre), he considered himself a sort of official functionary. After breakfast he asked us if we would like to hear him sing—sat down to the piano, accompanying himself very simply and easily and sang extremely well. I was much astonished and Mme. A. was delighted, especially when he sang some old-fashioned songs from the "Dame Blanche" and the "Domino Noir." The old father was enchanted, a broad smile on his face. He confided to W. that he had hoped his son would walk in his footsteps and content himself with a modest position as architect in the country, but after six months in Paris where he had sent him to learn his profession his ideas had completely changed and he would not hear of vegetating in the country.

We had, too, sometimes a doctor from one of the neighbouring villages. He had married an Englishwoman. They had a nice house and garden and he often had English boys over in the summer to learn French. He brought them occasionally to us for tea and tennis, begging us not to speak English to them. But that was rather difficult, with the English terms at tennis—horses and dogs always spoken to in English. One could not speak French to a fox-terrier bred in Oxfordshire.

Another pretty, simple fête was the Blessing of the Flag given by Francis to the Pompiers of Montigny, our little village in the woods just above the château. My husband had always promised them a flag, but he died before their society was formed. Three years after his death, when we were living in the small place which now belongs to my son, a deputation arrived from Montigny one Sunday afternoon to ask if Francis would give the flag his father had promised. This of course he was delighted to do. He knew all the men and they all knew him—had seen him since he was a baby—all of them had worked in his father's woods, and two or three of the older ones had taken care of him and his gun when he first began to shoot.

His father gave him a gun when he was twelve years old—had it made at Purdy's in London, a reduced model of his own. No one is allowed to shoot in France till he is sixteen years old and then must have his "permis de chasse" duly signed by the Mayor. So it was rather difficult to get Francis and his gun into the woods—once there they were safe. Nothing would have induced him to let any of the men carry it. He walked beside the keeper with his gun over his shoulder just like him; they did meet two gendarmes one day and quickly the gun was given to some one else. I think the gendarmes quite realised the situation (Labbey, the keeper, said they knew all about it), but they were friends of the family, W.'s appointment, probably, and asked no questions.

A visit at the château.

It was necessary of course to consult the local authorities before deciding such an important question as the presentation of a flag to the Pompiers. Francis went over two or three days later and interviewed the curé, the Mayor and the school-master, found out where the flag must be ordered in Paris and decided the day a fortnight later, a Sunday, of course. The function was to consist of a service and sermon at the church and a "vin d'honneur" offered by the Pompiers at the Mairie, which they hoped Madame Waddington would grace by her presence.

The flag was duly ordered, sent direct to Montigny and everything was ready on the appointed day. We had fine weather, a bright, cold November afternoon; the country looked beautiful, all the trees red and yellow, a black line of pines in the middle of the woods. The long straggling village street, ending at the church on the top of the hill, was full of people; all the children in the middle of the road, their mothers dashing after them when they heard the horn of the auto.

We were quite a large party, as the house was full, and we brought all our guests with us, including an American cousin, who was much interested in the local festivities. The Pompiers were drawn up in the court-yard of the Mairie, their beautiful new flag well to the front. Almost all were in uniform, and those who had not yet been able to get one wore a clean white shirt and the Pompier's red belt. There was a cheer and a broad smile on all their faces when we drove up. Francis got out, as he was to head the procession with the Mayor and the curé. We went on to the church and stationed ourselves on the steps of the Infant School to see the cortège arrive.

It was quite a pretty sight as it wound up the hill: first the banner of blue silk with gold cords, which was held proudly aloft by two tall young fellows, then Francis walking between the curé and the Mayor, the Pompiers immediately behind them, then the Municipal Council, the usual escort of children that always turns out on such occasions bringing up the rear. We let the procession pass into the church and then took our places; a front pew was reserved for the family, but Francis and I sat on two arm-chairs inside the chancel, just behind the Pompiers.

The fine old church, which is rather large for such a small village, was crowded; they told me many people had come from the neighbouring hamlets. The Montigny people had done their best to beautify their church; there were a few plants and flowers and some banners and draperies—church property, which always figured upon any great occasion. They told us with pride that the school-master had arranged the music. I suppose the poor man did what he could with the material he had, but the result was something awful. The chorister, a very old man, a hundred I should think, played the harmonium, which was as old as he was. It groaned and wheezed and at times stopped altogether. He started the cantique with a thin quavering voice which was then taken up by the school-children, particularly the boys who roared with juvenile patriotism and energy each time they repeated the last line, "pour notre drapeau, pour notre patrie."

The sermon was very good—short and simple. It was preached by the Doyen of Neuilly—a tall, strong, broad-shouldered man who would have seemed more at home in a dragoon's uniform than in the soutane. But he knew his business well, had a fine voice and very good delivery; his peroration and appeal to the men to "remember always that the flag was the symbol of obedience, of loyalty, of devotion, to their country and their God," was really very fine. I almost expected to hear cheers. The French are very emotional, and respond instantly to any allusion to country or flag. The uniform (even the Pompier's) has an enormous prestige. Then came the benediction, the flag held high over the kneeling congregation, and the ceremony was ended.

We stopped a few moments after the service to let the procession pass out and also to thank the preacher and one or two curés who had assisted on the occasion; they did not come to the "vin d'honneur."

We walked down to the Mairie, where the Mayor and his Adjoint were waiting for us; they conducted us to a large room upstairs where there was a table with champagne bottles, glasses and a big brioche. As soon as we had taken our places at the top of the room, the Pompiers and Municipal Council trouped in and Francis made quite a pretty little speech. It was the first time I had ever heard him speak in public; he did it very well, was not at all shy. Then there was a pause—the Mayor filled a glass of champagne, handed it to me, took one himself and we "trinqué'd" solemnly. Still there seemed a little hitch, no one else took any and there was an air of expectancy. I made a sign to the school-master, who was also the Adjoint, and he explained to me in a low voice that he thought it would give great pleasure if I would shake hands and trinquer with all the Pompiers. So I asked to have all the glasses filled and made the round, shaking hands with every one.

Some of them were very shy, could hardly make up their minds to put out their big, rough hands; some of the old ones were very talkative: "C'est moi qui suis Jacques, Madame, j'ai nettoyé le premier fusil de M. Francis." Another in a great hurry to get to me: "C'est moi qui ai remassé le premier lièvre de M. Francis," etc. I remember the "premier lièvre" quite well; Francis carried it home himself and dashed into his father's study swinging the poor beast by its long ears, the blood dripping from a hole in its neck. It was difficult to scold, the child was so enchanted, even old Ferdinand did not grumble but came to the rescue at once with brushes and "savon noir."

The wine had loosened the tongues and made every one more at ease. I asked that Hubert (our coachman who had been in W.'s service for thirty-one years) should be invited to come up and have a glass of champagne. He knew everybody, having driven W. about in his dog-cart all over the country. He was delighted to take part in the fête and made his little speech, saying he had seen Monsieur Francis when he was only a few hours old, and that he had *grown since*—which joke was received with great applause.

Then some of the young men went off with Francis to look at the automobile, a great novelty at that time. We went out and talked to the women who were waiting in the street. Every one looked smiling and pleased to see us; the men all formed again in procession and escorted us to the end of the street, the whole village naturally following. They stopped at the foot of the hill, giving us a ringing cheer as we left.

I never but once saw the whole neighbourhood assembled—when the only son of the Baron de L. married. The Baron and his wife were very good specimens of provincial *noblesse*. He was a tall, heavily-built man, square-shouldered, with the weather-beaten complexion of a man who spent all his days riding about his fields and woods; a pleasant, jovial manner, quite the type of the country gentleman.

They lived in a charming old Louis XV. château almost in the forest of Villers-Cotterets—their park touching the line of wood. They went rarely to Paris; lived almost all the year in the country and were devoted to their place. One just saw the pointed red roof of the château in the trees as one passed on the road. It stood high, a very steep road leading up to it. At the foot of the hill were market gardens, which made a very curious effect from a distance—the long rows of glass "cloches" making huge white spots. The vegetables always looked very tempting as we passed in the early summer. They were all "primeurs"—the gardens lying in full sun and were sent off to the Paris market. Half-way up the slope was a pretty little church almost hidden in the trees, and a tiny village struggled up the hill and along the road.

The bride, dressed in white—a slight girlish figure—was standing near her mother-in-law and had a pretty smile of welcome for all the guests. It was rather an ordeal for her, as she was a stranger in the country (she came from the south of France) and every one was looking at the newcomer.

It was in the first year of my marriage, my first appearance in the country, and I was rather puzzled about my dress for the occasion. We were asked to dinner at seven o'clock. My first idea was to wear full dress—light-blue satin and diamonds—but a niece of Mme. A.'s, who was staying with us and who had been to some entertainments in that part of the country, advised me strongly to dress more simply. "They would not understand that sort of toilette and I would be overdressed and probably uncomfortable." So I compromised with a high white dress, no diamonds and one string of pearls.

We had a short hour's drive. It was a clear, cold night and we saw the château from a great distance. It was brilliantly lighted. The lights twinkling through the trees looked like huge fireflies. As we drove into the rather small court-yard there was quite a stir of carriages arriving and backing out. The hall doors were wide open; a flood of light streaming out over the steps—Baron de L. and his son at the door. There was a hum of voices in the drawing-room and there seemed to be a great many people. The rooms were handsome—plenty of light, the old tapestry furniture looked very well, standing straight and stiff against the wall, and the number of people took away the bare unused look they generally had.

All the châteaux of the neighbourhood were represented: The Comte de Lubersac and his sister had come over from their fine place, Maucreux. He was a very handsome young man—a great hunter and master of hounds of the stag hunting in the forest of Villers-Cotterets; his sister, Mlle. de Lubersac, most attractive, with the face of a saint. She was very simply dressed in a high black dress. She lived almost the life of a Sister of Charity—going about all day among the sick and poor, but she had promised her father, who was a great invalid, almost crippled with gout, to remain with him as long as he lived. It was only after his death that she took the vows and entered one of the strictest orders (Carmelites) in France.

There were also the châtelaines of Thury en Valois—a fine château and estate, not very far from us in the other direction. They had splendid gardens and their fruit and vegetables were famous all over the country. Mme. de Thury was a compatriot—the daughter of an American general; the young Comte de Melun from Brumetz—very delicate looking, with a refined student's face. His father was a great friend of the Maréchal MacMahon and one of the leaders of the Catholic clerical party, and the young man was very religious. Their woods touched ours and once or twice when we were riding late, we saw him kneeling at a little old shrine, "the White Lady," which was almost hidden under the big trees—so little left that the ordinary passer-by would have seen nothing. There were also the owners of Colinance—rather an ugly square house standing low, surrounded by a marsh, but a good property—and three or four men I did not know—the bride's brother and one or two of her relations.

There was hardly time to introduce every one, as dinner was announced almost immediately. We were a large party, about twenty. All the women, except the bride and me, were dressed in black, high or a very little open—no lace, nor jewels. Henriette was right. I would have looked absurd if I had worn a low dress. The dinner was very good, very abundant and very long. The men said the wines were excellent. The talk was animated enough—it was principally the men who talked. I didn't think the women said much. I listened only, as I was too new in the country to be at all up in local topics.

After coffee the men went off to smoke and we women remained alone for some time. I wasn't sorry, as one had so few opportunities of seeing the neighbours, particularly the women, who rarely went out of their own places. One met the men hunting, or in the train, or at the notary's.

The notary is a most important person in all small country towns in France. Everybody consults him, from the big landowner when he has discussions with his neighbour over right of way, to the peasant who buys a few metres of land as soon as he has any surplus funds. We were constantly having rows with one of our neighbours over a little strip of wood that ran up into ours. Whenever he was angry with us, which happened quite often (we never knew why), he had a deep, ugly ditch made just across the road which we always took when we were riding around the property. The woods were so thick and low, with plenty of thorns, that we could not get along by keeping on one side and were obliged to go back and make quite a long détour. The notary did his best to buy it for us, but the man would never sell—rather enjoyed, I think, having the power to annoy us.

Mme. de Thury and I fraternised a little and I should have liked to see more of her, but soon after that evening they had great trouble. They had a great deal of illness and lost a son. I never saw Thury till after both of them were dead. The château had been sold, most of the furniture taken away and the whole place had a deserted, neglected look that made one feel quite miserable. The big drawing-room was piled up with straw, over the doors were still two charming dessus-de-porte, the colours quite fresh—not at all faded—chickens were walking about in another room, and upstairs in a pretty corner room, with a lovely view over woods and park, was a collection of photographs, engravings (one the mother of the late owner), a piece of unfinished tapestry, samplers, china vases, books, papers, two or three knots of faded ribbon, all tossed in a corner like a heap of rubbish. The things had evidently been forgotten in the big move, but it looked melancholy.

The château must have been charming when it was furnished and lived in. Quantities of rooms, a long gallery with small rooms on one side, the "garçonnière" or bachelors' quarters, led directly into the church, where many Thurys are sleeping their last sleep. The park was beautiful and there was capital shooting. W. had often shot there in the old days when their shooting parties were famous.

We ended our evening with music, the bride playing extremely well. Mme. de Thury also sang very well. She had learnt in Italy and sang in quite bravura style. The evening didn't last very long after the men came in. Everybody was anxious to get the long, cold drive over.

I enjoyed myself very much. It was my first experience of a French country entertainment and it was very different from what I had expected. Not at all stiff and a most cordial welcome. I thought—rather naïvely perhaps—that it was the beginning of many entertainments of the same kind, but I never dined out again in the country. It is only fair to say that we never asked any one to dine either. It was not the habit of the house, and I naturally fell into their ways. Luncheon was what people liked best, so as not to be too late on the road or to cross the forest after nightfall, when the darkness was sometimes impenetrable. Some of the châtelaines received once a week. On that day a handsome and plentiful luncheon was provided and people came from the neighbouring châteaux, and even from Paris, when the distance was not too great and the trains suited.

We had quite an excitement one day at the château. Francis was riding with the groom one morning about the end of August, and had hardly got out of the gates, when he came racing back to tell us that the manoeuvres were to take place very near us, small detachments of troops already arriving; and the village people had told him that quite a large contingent, men and horses, were to be quartered at the château. W. sent him straight off again to the mayor of Marolles—our big village—to know if his information was correct, and how many people we must provide for. Francis met the mayor on the road on his way to us, very busy and bustled with so many people to settle. He was billeting men and horses in the little hamlet, and at all the farms. He told us we were to have thirty men and horses—six officers, twenty-four men; and they would arrive at sundown, in time to cook their dinner. Hubert, the coachman, was quite bewildered at first how to provide for so many, but fortunately the stables and dependencies were very large, and it was quite extraordinary how quickly and comfortably everything was arranged. Men from the farm brought in large bundles of straw, and everybody lent a willing hand—they love soldiers in France, and are always proud and happy to receive them.

About 4.30, when we had just moved out to the tennis ground for tea, we saw an officer with his orderly riding up the avenue. He dismounted as soon as he caught sight of us sitting on the lawn, and introduced himself, said he was sent on ahead to see about lodging for himself, his brother-officers, and his men. They were part of a cavalry regiment, chasseurs, stationed at a small town in the neighbourhood. He asked W. if he might see the soldiers' quarters, said they brought their own food and would cook their dinner; asked if there was a room in the château where the sous-officiers could dine, as they never eat with their men. He, with W. and Francis, went off to inspect the arrangements and give the necessary orders. We had already seen to the officers' rooms, but hadn't thought of a separate dining-room for the sous-officiers; however, it was easily managed. We gave them the children's dining-room, in the wing near the kitchen and offices.

When W. came in he told us the whole party had arrived, and we started off to the communs to see what was going on. The stable-yard, which is very large, with some fine trees and outbuildings all around it, was filled with blue-coated soldiers and small chestnut horses—some were drinking out of the troughs; some, tied to the trees, and rings on the wall, were being rubbed down—the men walking about with the officers' valises and their own kits, undoing blankets, tin plates, and cups; and I should think every man and boy on our place and in the small hamlet standing about anxious to do something. Our little fox-terriers were mad with excitement; even the donkey seemed to feel there was something different in the air. He brayed noisily, and gave little vicious kicks occasionally when some of the horses passed too near. A group of officers was standing at the door of the stables talking to Hubert, who had managed very well, putting all the officers' horses into a second stable, which was always kept for guests, and the others in the various sheds and outhouses, all under cover.

W. introduced the officers—a nice-looking lot, chasseurs, in the light-blue uniform, which is so smart. He had asked permission for the men to dine at the château. They had their own meat and bread, but our chef was most anxious to cook it for them, and make them another substantial dish; so it was agreed that they should dine at six in the servants' hall. They all marched up in procession, headed by their sergeants; the blue tunics and red trousers looked very pretty as they came along the big avenue. The commandant asked W. if he would go and say a few words to them when they were having their coffee. They were very quiet; one hardly heard anything, though all the windows were open. W. said it was quite interesting to see all the young faces smiling and listening hard when he made his little speech. He asked them if they had had a good dinner; he hoped his man knew how to cook for soldiers. They all nodded and smiled at the chef, who was standing at the door looking very hot and very pleased. He had produced a sweet dish—I don't know what with, as he didn't habitually have thirty extra people to dinner—but I have always seen that when people *want* to do anything it is usually accomplished.

Our dinner was very pleasant. We were ten at table—W. and I, Henrietta, and a niece. The men talked easily, some of them Parisians, knowing every one. They knew that W. had remained at the château all during the Franco-German War, and were much interested in all he told them of the Prussian occupation. Only one of them had, as a very young fellow, served in 1870. All the rest were too young, and, like all young soldiers who have not been through a war and seen the horrors of it, were rather anxious to have their chance, and not spend all the best years of their lives in a small, dull garrison town.

Soldiers at the château.

We discussed the plans for the next day. They were going to have a sham fight over all the big fields in our neighbourhood, and advised us to come and see it. They said the best time would be about ten in the morning, when they were to monter à l'assaut of a large farm with moat and draw-bridge near Dammarie. They were to make a very early start (four o'clock), and said they would be very pleased to have some hot coffee before mounting, if it could be had at that unearthly hour. They were very anxious about choosing a horse out of their squadron for the general, who was an infantryman, very stout, very rheumatic, and a very bad rider. The horse must be sure-footed, an easy mouth, easy canter, no tricks, accustomed to drum and bugle, to say nothing of the musket-shots, etc.

Henrietta and I rather amused ourselves after dinner teaching the commandant and another officer halma, which was just then at the height of its popularity. We had brought it over from London, where the whole society was mad over it. We were staying in a country house one year where there were seven tables of halma in the long gallery. The gentlemen rather disdained it at first, but as the game went on and they began to realise that there was really some science in it, and that our men were placing themselves very comfortably in their little squares, while theirs were wandering aimlessly about the centre of the board, they warmed to their task, and were quite vexed when they were badly beaten. They wanted their revanche. W. came in and gave a word of advice every now and then. The others finished their billiards, came to look on, each one suggesting a different move, which, of course, only complicated matters, and they lost again. Then some of the others tried with the same result. I think we played five or six games. They were so much pleased with the game that they asked us to write down the name and where to get it, and one of them afterward told my nephew, also a cavalry officer, that they introduced it at their mess and played every night instead of cards or dominoes. It was really funny to see how annoyed they were when their scientific combinations failed. The next morning was beautiful—a splendid August day, not too hot, little white clouds scurrying over the bright blue sky, veiling the sun. We started about nine, W., Francis, and I riding, the others driving. There were a good many people about in the fields and cross-roads, a few farmers riding, and everybody wildly interested telling us which way to go. Janet, my American niece, who was staying in the country in France for the first time, was horrified to see women working in the fields, couldn't believe that her uncle would allow it on his farm, and made quite an appeal to him when we all got home, to put an end to such cruel proceedings. It seems women never work in the fields in America, except negresses on some of the Southern plantations. I have been so long away that I had forgotten that they didn't, and I remember quite well my horror the first time we were in Germany, when we saw a woman and an ox harnessed together.

We separated from the carriage at the top of the hill, as we could get a nice canter and shorter road across the fields. We soon came in sight of the farmhouse, standing low, with moat and drawbridge, in rather an isolated position in the middle of the fields, very few trees around it. There was no longer any water in the moat. It was merely a deep, wide, damp ditch with long, straggling vines and weeds filling it up, and a slippery, steep bank. Soldiers were advancing in all directions, the small infantrymen moving along with a light, quick step; the cavalry apparently had been on the ground some time, as they were all dismounted and their horses picketed. We didn't go very near, as W. wasn't quite sure how the horses would stand the bugle and firing. They were already pulling hard, and getting a little nervous. It was pretty to see the soldiers all mount when the bugle rang out, and in a moment the whole body was in motion. The rush of the soldiers over the wide plains and the drawbridge looked irresistible—the men swarmed down the bank and over the ditch—one saw a confused mass of red trousers and kepis. The cavalry came along very leisurely, guarding the rear. I looked for the general. He was standing with some of his staff on a small hill directing operations. He did look stout and very red and warm; however, it was the last day, so his troubles were over for the present.

One of the officers saw us and came up to pay his respects; said they wouldn't be back at the château until about five; perhaps the ladies would come to the stable-yard and see the pansage. It was quite interesting; all the horses ranged in a semi-circle, men scrubbing and combing hard, the sous-officiers superintending, the officers standing about smoking and seeing that everything was being packed and ready for an early start the next morning. I was astonished to see how small the horses were. My English horse, also a chestnut, was not particularly big, but he looked a giant among the others. They admired him very much, and one of the officers asked Hubert if he thought I would like to sell him.

Our dinner was again very pleasant, and we had more halma in the evening. W. played once or twice, and as he was a fairly good player, the adversaries had no chance. We broke up early, as they were to start again at some unearthly hour the next morning. It seems they were very lively in the stables after dinner—we heard sounds of merriment, singing, and choruses, and, I fancy, dancing. However, it made quite a pleasant break in our summer, and the big place seemed quieter and lonelier than ever after such unusual animation. W. said the war talk was much keener than the first day when they were smoking in the gallery; all the young ones so eager to earn their stripes, and so confident that the army had profited by its bitter experience during the Franco-German War.

Election day is always a very important day in France. The village farmers and labourers put on their best clothes—usually a black coat, silk hat and white shirt—and take themselves solemnly to the Mairie where the voting takes place. For weeks beforehand agents and lecturers come from Paris and bamboozle the simple village people with newspapers, money and wonderful promises. It is astounding how easily the French peasant believes all that the political agents tell him and all that he reads in the cheap papers, for, as a rule—taken en masse—they are very intelligent and at the same time suspicious (méfiants), manage their own little affairs very well and are rarely taken in; but there is something in the popular orator that carries them away and they really believe that a golden epoch is coming—when there will be no rich and no poor and plenty and equality for all. They don't care a bit what form of government they live under as long as their crops are good, and they can have regular work and no war. The political agitators understand that very well. They never lay any stress on Royalist or Bonapartist, or even a military candidate. The "People's Candidate" is always their cry—one of themselves who understands them and will give them all they want. They are disappointed *always*. The ministers and deputies change, but their lives don't, and run on in the same groove; but they are just as sanguine each time there is an election, convinced that, at last, the promised days of high pay and little work are coming.

I tried to reason with a nice, respectable man one day, the village mason—one of the most fiery orators at the café, over his dominoes, but in everyday life a sober, hardworking man, with a sickly wife and several children, who are all clothed and generally looked after by us. His favourite theme was the owners of châteaux and big houses who lived in luxury and thought nothing of the poor.

I said to him, "Why do you listen to all those foolish speeches that are made in the cafés? You know it isn't true half they say. Whenever you come and ask for anything for your wife and your children, it is always given to you. You know quite well whenever any one is ill in the village, they always come here for wine, old linen, or bouillon."

"Oh, oui, Madame is good, but Madame does not understand."

"But it is you, mon ami, who don't understand. Once the election is over, and they have got your vote, no one will think about you any more."

"Oh, yes, Madame, everything will be divided—there will be no more big houses, every one will have a garden and rabbits—not all for the rich. It is not right; Madame knows it is not right." It was quite useless talking to him.

Women in France never take the active part in elections that they do in England. It interested me so much when we were living in England to see many of the great ladies doing all they could for their candidate, driving all over the country, with his colours on servants and horses, a big bill in the windows of their carriages with "Vote for A." on it. In the drawing-room windows of a well-known society leader there were two large bills—"VOTE FOR A." I asked W. one day, when he was standing for the Senate, if he would like me to drive all about the country with his colours and "VOTE FOR WADDINGTON" on placards in the windows of the carriage; but he utterly declined any such intervention on my part, thought a few breakfasts at the château and a quiet talk over coffee and cigars would be more to the purpose. He never took much trouble over his elections the last years—meetings and speeches in all the small towns and "banquets de pompiers" were things of the past. He said the people had seen him "à l'oeuvre" and that no speeches would change a vote.

The only year that we gave ourselves any trouble was during the Boulanger craze. W. went about a great deal and I often went with him. The weather was beautiful and we rode all over the country. We were astounded at the progress "Boulangism" had made in our quiet villages. Wherever we went—in the cafés, in the auberges, in the grocer's shop—there was a picture of Boulanger prancing on his black horse.

We stopped one day at a miserable little cottage, not far from our place, where a workman had had a horrible accident—been caught in the machine of one of the sugar mills. Almost all the men in the village worked in W.'s woods and had always voted—as one man—for him or his friends. When we went into the poor little dark room, with literally nothing in it but the bed, a table, and some chairs, the first thing we saw was the well-known picture of Boulanger, on the mantelpiece. We talked a little to the man and his wife (the poor fellow was suffering terribly), and then W. said, "I am surprised to see that picture. Do you know General Boulanger? Have you ever seen him?" The man's face quite lighted up as he looked at the picture, and he answered: "Non, Monsieur, je ne l'ai jamais vu—mais il est crâne celui-là," and that was all that he could ever get out of him—"il est crâne." I don't know exactly what he meant. I don't think he knew himself, but he was quite excited when he spoke of the hero.

Boulanger's campaign was very cleverly done. His agents distributed papers, pictures and *money* most liberally. One of the curious features of that episode was the quantity of money that was given. Gold flowed freely in to the General's coffers from all parts of France; great names, grandes dames, giving largely and openly to the cause—a great deal sent anonymously and a great deal in very small sums.

Boulanger lived in our street, and I was astounded one day when I met him (I did not know him) riding—always with a man on each side of him. Almost every one took off his hat to him, and there were a few faint cries of "Vive Boulanger," proceeding chiefly from the painters and masons who were building a house just opposite ours.

Certainly for a short time he had the game in his hands—could, I think, have carried the country, but when the moment to act arrived, his nerve failed him. It is difficult to understand what made his great popularity. Politics had not been satisfactory. The President—Grévy—had resigned under unfortunate circumstances. There had been a succession of weak and inefficient cabinets, and there was a vague feeling of unrest in the country. Boulanger seemed to promise something better. He was a soldier (which always appeals to the French), young and dashing, surrounded by clever unscrupulous people of all classes. Almost all the young element of both parties, Radical and Conservative (few of the moderate Republicans), had rallied to his programme—"Révision et Dissolution." His friends were much too intelligent to let him issue a long "manifesto" (circular), promising all sorts of reforms and changes he never could have carried out, while his two catch words gave hopes to everybody. A revision of the constitution might mean a monarchy, empire, or military dictatorship. Each party thought its turn had come, and dissolving the chambers would of course bring a new one, where again each party hoped to have the majority.

The Paris election by an overwhelming majority was his great triumph. The Government did all they could to prevent it, but nothing could stop the wave of popularity. The night of the election Boulanger and his État-major were assembled at Durand's, the well-known café on the corner of the Boulevard and the rue Royale. As the evening went on and the returns came in—far exceeding anything they had hoped for—there was but one thought in every one's mind—"A l'Élysée." Hundreds of people were waiting outside and he would have been carried in triumph to the Palace. He could not make up his mind. At midnight he still wavered. His great friend, the poet Déroulède, then took out his watch—waited, in perfect silence, until it was five minutes past twelve, and then said, "Général, depuis cinq minutes votre auréole baisse." Boulanger went out by a side door, leaving his friends—disappointed and furious—to announce to the waiting crowd that the General had gone home. He could certainly have got to the Elysée that night. How long he would have stayed, and whom he would have put there, we shall never know.

MAREUIL, October 31st.

It has been a beautiful, warm, bright autumn day and, for a wonder, we have had no frost yet, not even a white one, so that the garden is still full of flowers, and all day the village children have been coming—begging for some to decorate the graves for to-morrow. I went in to the churchyard this afternoon, which was filled with women and children—looking after their dead. It is not very pretty—our little churchyard—part of a field enclosed on the slope of the hill, not many trees, a few tall poplars and a laurel hedge—but there is a fine open view over the great fields and woods—always the dark blue line of the forest in the distance. They are mostly humble graves—small farmers and peasants—but I fancy they must sleep very peacefully in the fields they have worked in all their lives—full of poppies and cornflowers in summer and a soft gold brown in the autumn, when the last crops are cut and the hares run wild over the hills.

I think these two days—the "Toussaint" and the "Jour des Morts"—are the two I like best in the Catholic Church, and certainly they are the only ones, in our part of the world, when the churches are full. I walked about some little time looking at all the preparations. Every grave had some flowers (sometimes only a faded bunch of the last field flowers) except one, where there were no flowers, but a little border of moss all around and a slip of pasteboard on a stick stuck into the ground with "à ma Mere" written on it. All the graves are very simple, generally a plain white cross with headstone and name. One or two of the rich farmers had something rather more important—a slab of marble, or a broken column when it was a child's grave, and were more ambitious in the way of flowers and green plants, but no show of any kind—none of the terrible bead wreaths one sees in large cities.

There was a poor old woman, nearly bent double, leaning on a stick, standing at one of the very modest graves; a child about six years old with her, with a bunch of flowers in a broken cup she was trying to arrange at the foot of the grave. I suppose my face was expressive, for the old woman answered my unspoken thought. "Ah, yes, Madame, it is *I* who ought to be lying there instead of my children. All gone before me except this one grandchild, and I a helpless, useless burden upon the charity of the parish."

On my way home I met all the village children carrying flowers. We had given our best chrysanthemums for the "pain bénit," which we offer to-morrow to the church. Three or four times a year, at the great fêtes, the most important families of the village offer the "pain bénit," which is then a brioche. We gave our boulanger "carte blanche," and he evidently was very proud of his performance, as he offered to bring it to us before it was sent to the church, but we told him we would see it there. I am writing late. We have all come upstairs. It is so mild that my window is open; there is not a sound except the sighing of the wind in the pines and the church bells that are ringing for the vigil of All Saints. Besides our own bells, we hear others, faintly, in the distance, from the little village of Neufchelles, about two miles off. It is a bad sign when we hear Neufchelles too well. Means rain. I should be so sorry if it rained to-morrow, just as all the fresh flowers have been put on the graves.

November 2nd. "Jour des Morts."

We had a beautiful day yesterday and a nice service in our little church. Our "pain bénit" was a thing of beauty and quite distracted the school children. It was a most imposing edifice—two large, round brioches, four smaller ones on top, they went up in a pyramid. The four small ones go to the notabilities of the village—the curé, two of the principal farmers and the miller; the whole thing very well arranged, with red and white flowers and lighted tapers. It was carried by two "enfants de choeur," preceded by the beadle with his cocked hat and staff and followed by two small girls with lighted tapers. The "enfants de choeur" were not in their festal attire of red soutanes and red shoes—only in plain black. Since the inventories ordered by the government in all the churches, most of the people have taken away their gifts in the way of vestments, soutanes, vases, etc., and the red soutanes, shoes and caps, with a handsome white satin embroidered vestment that C. gave the church when she was married, are carefully folded and put away in a safe place out of the church until better times should come.

After luncheon we went over to Soissons in the auto—the most enchanting drive through the forest of Villers-Cotterets—the poplar trees a line of gold and all the others taking the most lovely colours of red and brown. Soissons is a fine old cathedral town with broad squares, planted with stiff trees like all the provincial towns in France; many large old-fashioned hotels, entre cour et jardin, and a number of convents and abbeys, now turned into schools, barracks, government offices of all kinds, but the fine proportions and beautiful lines are always there.

The city has seen many changes since its first notoriety as the capital of the France of Clovis, and one feels how much has happened in the quiet deserted streets of the old town, where almost every corner is picturesque. The fine ruins of St. Jean des Vignes faced us as we drove along the broad boulevard. A façade and two beautiful towers with a cloister is all that remains of a fine old abbey begun in 1076. It is now an arsenal. One can not always get in, but the porter made no difficulty for us, and we wandered about in the courtyard and cloister. The towers looked beautifully grey and soft against the bright blue sky, and the view over Soissons, with all its churches and old houses, was charming. It seems that Thomas à Becket, Archbishop of Canterbury, lived at the Abbey when he was exiled from England and had taken refuge in France.

We wanted to go to the service in the Cathedral, but thought we would go first to the pâtissier (an excellent one, well known in all the neighbourhood) famous for a very good bonbon made of coffee and called "Tors de Soissons." The little place was full—every schoolboy in Soissons was there eating cakes and bonbons. There was a notice up in the shop, "Lipton Tea," and we immediately asked for some. The woman made a place for us, with difficulty, on a corner of a table and gave us very good English tea, toast and cakes. I complimented the patronne on her tea and she said so many automobiles with foreigners—English principally—passed through Soissons in the summer—all asking for tea—that she thought she must try to get some. One of the ladies told her where to get Lipton Tea and how much to pay for it. She has found it a very good speculation.

We walked to the Cathedral through a grand old Square planted with fine trees, that had once been a part of the garden of the Évêché. As it was getting dark, we could not see the outside very well. A gigantic mass of towers and little steeples loomed up through the twilight, but the inside was very striking—crowded with people, lights, banners, flowers everywhere—five or six priests were officiating and the Bishop in full dress, with his gold mitre on his head, was seated on his red velvet throne under the big crucifix. The congregation (there were a good many men) was following the service very devoutly, but there were a great many people walking about and stopping at the different chapels which rather takes away from the devotional aspect. Unfortunately the sermon had only just begun, so we didn't hear any music. The organ is very fine and they have a very good choir. Neither did we hear the famous chimes, which we regretted very much. Some of the bells have a beautiful sound—one in particular, that used to be at St. Jean de Vignes, has a wonderful deep note. One hears it quite distinctly above all the others. All the bells have names. This one used to be called "Simon," after a Bishop Simon le Gras, who blessed it in 1643. When the voice got faint and cracked with age, it was "refondue" (recast) and called Julie Pauline.

It was quite dark and cold when we started back. We had to light our big lantern almost as soon as we left Soissons. For some little time after we got out of the town we met people walking and driving—all with holiday garbs and faces—but once we plunged in the long forest alleys we were absolutely cut off from the outside world. It is a curious sensation I have never got accustomed to, those long, dark, lonely forest roads. The leaves were still so thick on the trees that we could hardly see the last glow of a beautiful orange sunset. The only sign of life was a charbonnier's hut in a clearing quite close to the road. They had a dull light; just enough to let us see dusky figures moving about.

This morning our church looked quite different—no more banners, embroideries or bright flowers, all draped in black and a bier covered with a black pall in the middle of the aisle—the curé in a black satin vestment; all the congregation in black. I went out before the end of the service. All the black draperies and the black kneeling figures and the funeral psalms were so inexpressibly sad and dreary. I was glad to get out into the sunshine and to the top of the hill, where the cemetery gates stood wide open and the sun was streaming down on all the green graves with their fresh flowers and plants. Soon we heard the sound of the chaunt, and the procession wound slowly up the steep, straggling village street. A banner and cross carried by the boys and girls—then the curé, with his "ostensoir," followed by his "enfants de choeur" carrying books and tapers, then the congregation. There were a great many people already in the cemetery. The little procession halted at the foot of the cross in the middle. There were several prayers and psalms, and then the curé made the tour of the cemetery, sprinkling all the graves with holy water and saying a short prayer at each. The procession broke up into groups, all kneeling at the different graves praying for their dead. There were not many men; a few old ones. They were not kneeling, but stood reverently, with bowed heads, when the curé passed. It was a pretty sight—the kneeling figures, the flower-covered graves, the little procession winding in and out among the tombstones, the white soutanes of the boys shining in the sun and not a sound except the droning of the chaunts. As it was fête—one of the great religious fêtes of the year—there was no work going on—no labourers in the fields, no carts on the road—nothing but the great stillness of the plains.

We had our curé at dinner. We were quite sure no one else would ask him and it seemed a shame to leave him in his empty "presbytère" on a fête day. I think his evenings with us are the only bright spots in his life just now. The situation of the priests is really wretched and their future most uncertain. This government has taken away the very small stipend they allowed them. Our curé got his house and nine hundred francs a year—not quite two hundred dollars. In many cases they have refused to let the priests live in their "presbytères" unless they pay rent. The churches are still open. They can have their services if they like, but those who have no fortune (which is the case with most of them) are entirely dependent upon the voluntary contribution of their parishioners.

Our little curé has no longer his servant—the traditional, plain, middle-aged bonne of the priest (they are not allowed to have a woman servant under fifty). He lives quite alone in his cold, empty house and has a meal of some kind brought into him from the railway café. What is hardest for him is never to have an extra franc to give to his poor. He is profoundly discouraged, but does his duty simply and cheerfully; looks after the sick, nurses them when there is a long illness or an accident, teaches the women how to keep their houses clean and how to cook good plain food. He is a farmer's son and extraordinarily practical. He came to us one day to ask if we had a spare washing tub we could give him. He was going to show a woman who sewed and embroidered beautifully and who was very poor and unpractical, how to do her washing. I think the people have a sort of respect for him, but they don't come to church. Everybody appeals to him. We couldn't do anything one day with a big kite some one had given the children. No one could in the house, neither gardener, chauffeur, nor footmen, so we sent for him, and it was funny to see him shortening the tail of the kite and racing over the lawn in his black soutane. However, he made it work.

He was rather embarrassed this evening, as he had refused something I had asked him to do and was afraid I wouldn't understand. We were passing along the canal the other day when the "éclusier" came out of his house and asked me if I would come and look at his child who was frightfully ill—his wife in despair. Without thinking of my little ones at home, I went into the house, where I found, in a dirty, smelly room, a slatternly woman holding in her arms a child, about two years old, who, I thought, was dead—such a ghastly colour—eyes turned up; however, the poor little thing moaned and moved and the woman was shaken with sobs—the father and two older children standing there, not knowing what to do. They told me the doctor had come in the early morning and said there was nothing to do. I asked if they had not sent for the curé. "No, they hadn't thought of it." I said I would tell him as I passed the presbytère on my way home. He wasn't there, but I left word that the child was dying—could he go?

The child died about an hour after I had left the house. I sent a black skirt to the woman and was then obliged to go to Paris for two or three days. When I came back I asked my gardener, who is from this part of the country and knows everybody, if the child's funeral had been quite right. He told me it was awful—there was no service—the curé would not bury him as he had never been baptized. The body had been put into a plain wooden box and carried to the cemetery by the father and a friend.

I was very much upset, but, of course, the thing was over and there was nothing to be done. However, when we talked it over, I understood quite well. To begin with, all priests are forbidden to read the burial service over any one who has not been baptized, therefore he had no choice. And this man was not only an unbeliever, but a mocker of all religion. When his last child was born he had friends over, from some of the neighbouring villages, who were Freemasons (they are a very bad lot in France); they had a great feast and baptized the child in red wine. I rather regretted the black frock I sent the mother, but she looked so utterly wretched and perhaps she could not help herself.

The little curé is very pleased to have his midnight mass this year on Christmas eve. Last year it was suppressed. There was such angry feeling and hostility to the clergy that the authorities were afraid there might be scenes and noisy protestations in the churches; perhaps in some quarters of the big cities, but certainly not in the country where people hold very much to the midnight mass. It is also one of the services that most people attend. It is always a pretty sight in the country, particularly if there happens to be snow on the ground. Every one that can walk comes. One sees the little bands arriving across the fields and along the canal—five or six together, with a lantern. Entire families turn out—the old grandfathers hobbling along on their sticks, the women carrying their babies, who are generally very good—quite taken up with the lights and music, or else asleep. We always sing Adam's "Noël." In almost every church in France, I think, they sing it. Even in the big Paris churches like the Madeleine and St. Eustache, where they have orchestras and trained choirs, they always sing the "Noël" at some period of the service.

MAREUIL, le 24 Mai.

To-day was the Première Communion at La Ferté, and I had promised the Abbé Devigne to go. I couldn't have the auto, as Francis was at a meeting of a Syndicat Agricole in quite another direction. So I took the train (about seven minutes), and I really believe I had the whole train to myself. No one travels in France, on

Sunday, in the middle of the day. It is quite a long walk from the station to the church (the service was at Notre Dame, the church on the hill), with rather a steep climb at the end. The little town looked quite deserted—a few women standing at their doors and in all directions white figures of all ages were galloping up the hill. The bells were ringing and we were a little late. The big doors of the church were wide open, the organ playing, and a good many people standing about. The altar was bright with flowers and candles, and "oriflammes" of blue and pink gauze, worked with gold and silver lilies, were stretched across the church between the pillars. One or two banners with the head of the Virgin and flowers painted in bright colours were also hanging from the columns. Two or three priests, with handsome vestments—white embroidered in gold—were officiating, and the choir boys wore their red petticoats—soutanes trimmed with lace and red shoes and caps. The Suisse (beadle), with his cocked hat, silver embroidered coat and big cane, was hovering about, keeping order.

Just inside the chancel sat the "communiants" —fifty boys and girls. The girls—all in white from top to toe—white dresses, shoes, and gloves, and long white veils coming to the edge of the dress, and either a white cap (which looks very pretty and quaint on the little heads—rather like some of the old Dutch pictures) or a wreath of white flowers. With them sat about half a dozen smaller girls—also in white, with wreaths of white roses. They were too small to make their first communion, but they were to hold the cordons of the banner when the procession passed down the church. The boys were all in black, short jackets, white waistcoats, and white ribbon bows on their sleeves.

The church was very full—mostly women, a few men at the bottom. It was a pretty sight when the procession moved around the church. First came the "sacristain" in his black skirt and white soutane, then the banner held by two of the big girls; the group of little ones—some of them quite tiny and so pretty with the wreaths of white roses on their black hair—holding the cords and looking most pleased with their part of the function. Just behind them came the good old religieuse Sœur St. Antoine, hovering over her little flock and keeping them all in their places; then all the communiants, the smallest girls first, the boys behind, all carrying lighted tapers and singing a hymn to the accompaniment of the organ.

They went first to the font, stopped there, and one of the girls read a sort of prayer renewing their baptismal vows. Then they started again, in the same order, to the Chapelle de la Vierge, always singing their hymn, and knelt at the rails. Then the hymn stopped, and they recited, all together, a prayer to the Virgin. The little childish voices sounded quite distinctly in the old church—one heard every word. The congregation was much interested.

There wasn't a sound. I don't know if it was any sort of religious feeling—some dim recollection of their early days, or merely the love of a show of any kind that is inherent in all the Latin race, but they seemed much impressed. While the collection was being made there was music—very good local talent—two violin soli played by a young fellow, from one of the small neighbouring châteaux, whom we all knew well, and the "Panus Angelicus" of César Franck, very well sung by the wife of the druggist. The curé of La Ferté, a very clever, cultivated man, with a charming voice and manner, made a very pretty, short address, quite suited to childish ears and understanding, with a few remarks at the end to the parents, telling them it was their fault if their children grew up hostile or indifferent to religion; that it was a perfectly false idea that to be patriotic and good citizens meant the abandonment of all religious principles.

We waited until the end of the service (Francis and his friends arrived in time to hear the curé's address), and watched the procession disappear down the steep path and gradually break up as each child was carried off by a host of friends and relations to its home. The curé was very pleased, said he had had a "belle fête"—people had sent flowers and ribbons and helped as much as they could to decorate the church. I asked him if he thought it made a lasting impression on the children. He thought it did on the girls, but the boys certainly not. Until their first communion he held them a little, could interest them in books and games after school hours, but after that great step in their lives they felt themselves men, and were impatient of any control.

VI

CHRISTMAS IN THE VALOIS

It had been a cold December, quite recalling Christmas holidays at home—when we used to think Christmas without snow wasn't a real Christmas, and half the pleasure of getting the greens to dress the church was gone, if the children hadn't to walk up to their ankles in untrodden snow across the fields to get the long, trailing branches of ivy and bunches of pine. We were *just* warm enough in the big château. There were two calorifères, and roaring wood fires (trees) in the chimneys; but even I must allow that the great stone staircase and long corridors were cold: and I couldn't protest when nearly all the members of the household—of all ages—wrapped themselves in woolen shawls and even fur capes at night when the procession mounted the big staircase. I had wanted for a long time to make a Christmas Tree in our lonely little village of St. Quentin, near Louvry, our farm, but I didn't get much support from my French friends and relations. W. was decidedly against it. The people wouldn't understand—had never seen such a thing; it was entirely a foreign importation, and just beginning to be understood in the upper classes of society. One of my friends, Madame Casimir-Périer,[4] who has a beautiful château at Pont-sur-Seine (of historic renown—"La Grande Mademoiselle" danced there—"A Pont j'ai fait venir les violons," she says in her memoirs), also disapproved. She gives away a great deal herself, and looks after all her village, but not in that way. She said I had much better spend the money it would cost, on good, sensible, warm clothes, blankets, "bons de pain," etc.; there was no use in giving them ideas of pleasure and refinement they had never had—and couldn't appreciate. Of course it was all perfectly logical and sensible, but I did so want to be unreasonable, and for once give these poor, wretched little children something that would be a delight to them for the whole year—one poor little ray of sunshine in their gray, dull lives.

We had many discussions in the big drawing-room after dinner, when W. was smoking in the arm-chair and disposed to look at things less sternly than in bright daylight. However, he finally agreed to leave me a free hand, and I told him we should give a warm garment to every child, and to the very old men and women. I knew I should get plenty of help, as the Sisters and Pauline promised me dolls and "dragées." I am sorry he couldn't be here; the presence of the Ambassador would give more éclat to the fête, and I think in his heart he was rather curious as to what we could do, but he was obliged to go back to London for Christmas. His leave

[4] Madame Casimir-Périer, widow of the well-known liberal statesman, and mother of the ex-President of the Republic.

was up, and beside, he had various country and shooting engagements where he would certainly enjoy himself and see interesting people. I shall stay over Christmas and start for London about the 29th, so as to be ready to go to Knowsley[5] by the 30th, where we always spend the New Year's Day.

We started off one morning after breakfast to interview the school-mistress and the Mayor—a most important personage. If you had ever seen St. Quentin you would hardly believe it could possess such an exalted functionary. The village consists of about twelve little, low gray houses, stretching up a steep hill, with a very rough road toward the woods of Borny behind. There are forty inhabitants, a church, and a school-house; but it *is* a "commune," and not the smallest in France (there is another still smaller somewhere in the South, toward the Alpes Maritimes). I always go and make a visit to the Mayor, who is a very small farmer and keeps the drinking shop[6] of the village. We shake hands and I sit a few minutes in a wooden chair in the one room (I don't take a drink, which is so much gained), and we talk about the wants and general behaviour of the population. The first time I went I was on horseback, so we dismounted and had our little talk. When we got up to go he hurriedly brought out a bench for me to mount from, and was quite bewildered when he saw W. lift me to the saddle from the ground.

The church is a pretty, old gray building—standing very high, with the little graveyard on one side, and a grass terrace in front, from which one has the most lovely view down the valley, and over the green slopes to the woods—Borny and Villers-Cotterets on one side, Chézy the other. It is very worn and dilapidated inside, and is never open except on the day of St. Quentin,[7] when the curé of La Ferté-Milon comes over and has a service. The school-house is a nice modern little house, built by W. some years ago. It looks as if it had dropped down by mistake into this very old world little hamlet.

It is a short walk, little more than two kilomètres from the gates of the big park, and the day was enchanting—cold and bright; too bright, indeed, for the low, gray clouds of the last days had been promising snow and I wanted it so much for my tree! We were quite a party—Henrietta, Anne, Pauline, Alice and Francis, Bonny the fox-terrier, and a very large and heavy four-wheeled cart, which the children insisted upon taking and which naturally had to be drawn up all the hills by the grown-ups, as it was much too heavy for the little ones. Bonny enjoyed himself madly, making frantic excursions to the woods in search of rabbits, absolutely unheeding call or whistle, and finally emerging dirty and scratched, stopping at all the rabbit holes he met on the way back, and burrowing deep into them until nothing was left but a stumpy little white tail wagging furiously.

We went first to the Mayor, as we were obliged to ask his permission to give our party at the school. Nothing in France can be done without official sanction. I wanted, too, to speak to him about a church service, which I was very anxious to have before the Tree was lighted. I didn't want the children's only idea of Christmas to be cakes and toys; and that was rather difficult to arrange, as the situa-

[5] The Earl of Derby's fine palace near Liverpool.

[6] Cabaret.

[7] In August, I think.

tion is so strained between the clergy and the laïques, particularly the curé and the school-master. I knew I should have no trouble with the school-mistress (the school is so small it is mixed—girls and boys from four to twelve—and there is a woman teacher; she is the wife of one of our keepers, and a nice woman)—but I didn't know how the Mayor would feel on the subject. However, he was most amiable; would do anything I wanted. I said I held very much to having the church open and that I would like as many people to come as it would hold. Would he tell all the people in the neighbourhood? I would write to the principal farmers, and I was sure we could make a most interesting fête. He was rather flattered at being consulted; said he would come up with us and open the church. It was absolutely neglected and there was nothing in the way of benches, carpets, etc. I told him I must go first to the school, but I would meet him at the church in half an hour.

The children were already up the hill, tugging the big cart filled with pine cones. The school-mistress was much pleased at the idea of the Christmas Tree; she had never seen one except in pictures, and never thought she would really have one in her school. We settled the day, and she promised to come and help arrange the church. Then we went into the school-room, and it was funny to hear the answer—a roar—of "Oui, Madame Waddington," when I asked her if the children were "good"; so we told them if they continued very good there would be a surprise for them. There are only thirty scholars—rather poor and miserable looking; some of them come from so far, trudge along the high-road in a little band, in all weathers, insufficiently clad—one big boy to-day had on a linen summer jacket. I asked the teacher if he had a tricot underneath. "Mais non, Madame, où l'aurait-il trouvé?" He had a miserable little shirt underneath which may once have been flannel, but which was worn threadbare.

We chose our day and then adjourned to the church, where the Mayor and a nice, red-cheeked, wrinkled old woman[8] who keeps the ornaments, such as they are, of the church were waiting for us. It was certainly bare and neglected, the old church, bits of plaster dropping off walls and ceilings, and the altar and one or two little statues still in good condition; but we saw we could arrange it pretty well with greens, the few flowers, chrysanthemums, Christmas roses, etc., that were still in the green-house, a new red carpet for the altar steps, and of course vases, tall candlesticks, etc. There was one handsome bit of old lace on a white nappe for the altar, and a good dress for the Virgin. We could have the school benches, and the Mayor would lend chairs for the "quality." On the whole we were satisfied, and told W. triumphantly at dinner that the Mayor, so far from making any objection, was pleased as Punch; he had never seen a Christmas Tree either.

---

[8] La Mère Rogov.

The Mayor and a nice, red-cheeked, wrinkled old woman were waiting for us.

The next day the list of the children was sent according to age and sex—also the old people; and we were very busy settling what we must do in the way of toys. The principal thing was to go to Paris and get all we wanted—toys, "bêtises", and shiny things for the Tree, etc. Henrietta and I undertook that, and we went off the same day that W. left for London. It was bitterly cold—the ground frozen hard—and we had a long drive, eighteen kilomètres through Villers-Cotterets forest—but no snow, only a beautiful white frost—all the trees and bushes covered with rime. It was like driving through a fairy forest. When we had occasional gleams of sunlight every leaf sparkled, and the red berries of the holly stood out beautifully from all the white. The fine old ruins of La Ferté looked splendid rising out of a mass of glistening underwood and long grass. We are very proud of our old château-fort, which has withstood well the work of time. It was begun (and never finished) by Louis d'Orléans in 1303, and was never inhabited. Now there is nothing left but the façade and great round towers, but quite enough to show what it might have been. There is also a bas-relief, perfectly well preserved, over the big door, of the Coronation of the Virgin, the kneeling figure quite distinct. On the other side is a great grass place (village green) where the fêtes of La Ferté take place, and where all the town dances the days of the "Assemblée." From the bottom of the terrace, at the foot of the low wall, one has a magnificent view over the town and the great forest of Villers-Cotterets stretching away in front, a long blue line on the horizon. In the main street of La Ferté there is a statue of Racine, who was born there. It is in white marble, in the classic draperies of the time, and is also in very good preservation. The baptismal register of Jean Racine is in the archives of La Ferté.

The road all the way to Villers-Cotterets was most animated. It was market-day, and we met every description of vehicle, from the high, old-fashioned tilbury of the well-to-do farmer, to the peasant's cart—sometimes an old woman driving, well wrapped up, her turban on her head, but a knit shawl wound around it, carrying a lot of cheeses to market; sometimes a man with a cow tied behind his cart, and a calf inside. We also crossed Menier's équipage de chasse, horses and dogs being exercised. We talked a few minutes to Hubert, the piqueur, who was in a very bad humor. They had not hunted for some days, and dogs and horses were unruly. The horses were a fine lot, almost all white or light gray. We go sometimes to the meets, and the effect is very good, as the men all wear scarlet coats and the contrast is striking.

We had an exhausting day in Paris, but managed to get pretty nearly everything. The little children were easily disposed of—dolls, drums, wooden horses, etc.; but the bigger boys and girls, who have outgrown toys, are more difficult to suit. However, with knives, paint-boxes, lotos (geographical and historical), for the boys; and handkerchief and work-boxes, morocco bags, etc., we did finally get our fifty objects. There are always extra children cropping up. Shopping was not very easy, as the streets and boulevards were crowded and slippery. We had a fairly good cab, but the time seemed endless. The big bazaars—Hôtel de Ville, rue d'Amsterdam, etc.—were the most amusing; really, one could get anything from a five-sou doll to a ménagère (the little cooking-stove all the peasant women use in their cottages). There were armies of extras—white-aproned youths, who did their best for us. We explained to one of the superintendents what we wanted, and he gave us a very intelligent boy, who followed us about with an enormous basket, into which everything was put. When we finally became almost distracted with the confusion and the crowd and our list, we asked the boy what he had liked when he was eleven years old at school; and he assured us all boys liked knives and guns.

When we had finished with the boys we had the decorations for the Tree to get, and then to the Bon Marché for yards of flannel, calico, bas de laine, tricots, etc. We had given W. rendezvous at five at Henrietta's. He was going to cross at night. We found him there having his tea. He had seen lots of people; been to the Élysée and had a long interview with the President (Grévy); then to the Quai d'Orsay to get his last instructions from the Minister; and he had still people coming to see him. When we left (our train was before his) he was closeted with one of his friends, a candidate for the Institute, very keen about his vote which W. had promised him, and going over for about the twentieth time the list of the members to see what his chances were. However, I suppose all candidates are exactly alike, and W. says he is sure he was a nuisance to all his friends when he presented himself at the Institute. One or two people were waiting in the dining-room to speak to him, and his servant was distracted over his valise, which wasn't begun then. I promised him I would write him a faithful account of our fête once we had decided our day. We took the five-o'clock train down, and a nice cold drive we had going home. The roads were rather slippery, and the forest black and weird. The trees which had been so beautiful in the morning covered with rime, seemed a massive black wall hemming us in. It is certainly a lonely bit of country, once we had left the lights of Villers-Cotterets behind us, crossed the last railway, and were fairly started in the forest. We didn't meet anything—neither cart, carriage, bûcheron, nor pedestrian of any kind.

Henrietta was rather nervous, and she breathed a sigh of relief when we got out on the plains and trotted down the long hill that leads to La Ferté. The château lights looked very warm and home-like as we drove in. We gave a detailed account of all we had bought, and as we had brought our lists with us we went to work at once, settling what each child should have. I found a note from the Abbé Maréchal, the curé of Laferté-Milon, whom I wanted to consult about our service. He is a very clever, moderate man, a great friend of ours, and I was sure he would help us and arrange a service of some kind for the children. Of course I was rather vague about a Catholic service; a Protestant one I could have arranged myself, with some Christmas carols and a short liturgy, but I had no idea what Christmas meant to Catholic minds. We had asked him to come to breakfast, and we would go over to the village afterward, see the church and what could be done. He was quite pleased at the idea of doing anything for his poor little parish, and he is so fond of children and young people that he was quite as much interested as we were. He knew the church, having held a service there three or four times. We walked over, talking over the ceremony and what we could do. He said he would give a benediction, bring over the Enfant Jésus, and make a small address to the children. The music was rather difficult to arrange, but we finally agreed that we would send a big omnibus to bring over the harmonium from La Ferté, one or two Sisters, two choir children, and three or four of the older girls of the school who could sing, and he would see that they learned two or three canticles.

We agreed to do everything in the way of decoration. He made only one condition: that the people should come to the service. I could answer for all our household and for some of the neighbours—almost all, in fact—as I was sure the novelty of the Christmas Tree would attract them, and they wouldn't mind the church service thrown in.

We went of course to see the Mayor, as the curé was obliged to notify him that he wished to open the church, and also to choose the day. We took Thursday, which is the French holiday; that left us just two days to make our preparations. We told Madame Isidore (the school-mistress) we would come on Wednesday for the church, bringing flowers, candles, etc., and Thursday morning to dress the Tree. The service was fixed for three o'clock—the Tree afterward in the school-room. We found our big ballots[9] from the bazaars and other shops, when we got home, and all the evening we wrote tickets and names (some of them so high-sounding—Ismérie, Aline, Léocadie, etc.), and filled little red and yellow bags, which were very troublesome to make, with "dragées."

Wednesday we made a fine expedition to the woods—the whole party, the donkey-cart, and one of the keepers to choose the Tree—a most important performance, as we wanted the real pyramid "sapin," tapering off to a fine point at the top. Labbey (keeper) told us his young son and the coachman's son had been all the morning in the woods getting enormous branches of pine, holly, and ivy, which we would find at the church. We came across various old women making up their bundles of fagots and dead wood (they are always allowed to come once a week to pick up the dead wood, under the keeper's surveillance). They were principally from Louvry and St. Quentin, and were staggering along, carrying quite heavy bundles on their poor old bent backs. However, they were very smiling to-day, and I think the burden was lightened by the thought of the morrow. We found a fine tree, which was installed with some difficulty in the donkey-cart; Francis and Alice taking turns driving, perched on the trunk of the tree, and Labbey walking behind, supporting the top branches.

We found the boys at the church, having already begun their decorations—enormous, high pine branches ranged all along the wall, and trails of ivy on the windows. The maids had arrived in the carriage, bringing the new red carpet, vases, candelabras and tall candlesticks, also two splendid wax candles painted and decorated, which Gertrude Schuyler had brought us from Italy; all the flowers the gardener would give them, principally chrysanthemums and Christmas roses. It seems he wasn't at all well disposed; couldn't imagine why "ces dames" wanted to despoil the green-houses "pour ce petit trou de St. Quentin."

[9] Big packages.

There was one handsome bit of old lace on a white nappe for the altar.

We all worked hard for about an hour, and the little church looked quite transformed. The red carpet covered all the worn, dirty places on the altar steps, and the pine branches were so high and so thick that the walls almost disappeared. When the old woman (gardienne) appeared she was speechless with delight! As soon as we had finished there, we adjourned to the school-house, and to our joy snow was falling—quite heavy flakes. Madame Isidore turned all the children into a small room, and we proceeded to set up our Tree. It was a great deal too tall, and if we hadn't been there they would certainly have chopped it off at the top, quite spoiling our beautiful point; but as we insisted, they cut away from the bottom, and it really was the regular pyramid one always wants for a Christmas Tree. We put it in a big green case (which we had obtained with great difficulty from the gardener; it was quite empty, standing in the orangerie, but he was convinced we would never bring it back), moss all around it, and it made a great effect. The "garde de Borny" arrived while we were working, and said he would certainly come to the church in his "tenue de garde"; our two keepers would also be there.

Thursday morning we went early (ten o'clock) to St. Quentin and spent over two hours decorating the Tree, ticketing and arranging all the little garments. Every child in the neighbourhood was hanging around the school-house when we arrived, the entrance being strictly forbidden until after the service, when the Tree would be lighted. I expressed great surprise at seeing the children at the school on a holiday, and there were broad grins as they answered, "Madame Waddington nous a dit de venir." It had snowed all night, and the clouds were low and gray, and looked as if they were still full of snow. The going was extremely difficult; not that the snow was very deep, but there was enough to make the roads very slippery. We had the horses "ferrés à glace," and even the donkey had nails on his shoes. The country looked beautiful—the poor little village quite picturesque, snow on all the dark roofs, and the church standing out splendidly from its carpet of snow—the tall pines not quite covered, and always the curtain of forest shutting in the valley.

We left the maids to breakfast with the keeper, and promised to be back at three o'clock punctually. Our coachman, Hubert, generally objects strongly to taking out his horses in bad weather on rough country roads and making three or four trips backward and forward; but to-day he was quite serene. He comes from that part of the neighbourhood and is related to half the village. Our progress was slow, as we stopped a good deal. It was a pretty sight as we got near St. Quentin: the church, brightly lighted, stood out well on the top of the hill against a background of tall trees, the branches just tipped with snow. The bell was ringing, the big doors wide open, sending out a glow of warmth and colour, and the carpet of white untrodden country snow was quite intact, except a little pathway made by the feet of the men who had brought up the harmonium. The red carpet and bright chrysanthemums made a fine effect of colour, and the little "niche" (it could hardly be called a chapel) of the Virgin was quite charming, all dressed with greens and white flowers, our tall Italian candles making a grand show.

The La Ferté contingent had arrived. They had much difficulty in getting the omnibus up to the church, as it was heavy with the harmonium on top; however, everybody got out and walked up the hill, and all went off well. The Abbé was robing, with his two choir children, in the minute sacristy, and the two good Sisters were standing at the gate with all their little flock—about ten girls, I should think. There were people in every direction, of all sizes and ages—some women carrying a baby in their arms and pushing one or two others in a cart, some wretched old people so bent and wrinkled one couldn't imagine how they could crawl from one room to another. A miserable old man bent double, really, leaning on a child and walking with two canes, was pointed out to me as the "père Colin," who makes the "margottins" (bundles of little dry sticks used for making the fires) for the château. However, they were all streaming up the slippery hill-side, quite unmindful of cold or fatigue. We walked up, too, and I went first to the school-house to see if our provisions had come. Food was also a vexed question, as tea and buns, which would seem natural to us, were unknown in these parts. After many consultations with the women about us—lessiveuses (washerwomen), keepers' wives, etc.—we decided upon hot wine and brioches. The Mayor undertook to supply the wine and the glasses, and we ordered the brioches from the Hôtel du Sauvage at La Ferté; the son of the house is a very good pâtissier. It is a funny, old-fashioned little hotel, not very clean, but has an excellent cuisine, also a wonderful sign board—a bright red naked savage, with feathers in his hair and a club in his hand—rather like the primitive pictures of North American Indians in our school-books.

Everything was there, and the children just forming the procession to walk to the church. Some of the farmers' wives were also waiting for us at the school-house, so I only had a moment to go into the big class-room to see if the Tree looked all right. It was quite ready, and we agreed that the two big boys with the keeper should begin to light it as soon as the service was over. Madame Isidore (the school-mistress) was rather unhappy about the quantity of people. There were many more than thirty children, but Henrietta and Pauline had made up a bundle of extras, and I was sure there would be enough. She told us people had been on the way since nine in the morning—women and children arriving cold and wet and draggled, but determined to see everything. She showed me one woman from Chézy, the next village (some distance off, as our part of the country is very scantily populated; it is all great farms and forests; one can go miles without seeing a trace of habitation). She had arrived quite early with two children, a boy and a girl of seven and eight, and a small baby in her arms; and when Madame Isidore remonstrated, saying the fête was for her school only, not for the entire country-side, the woman answered that Madame always smiled and spoke so nicely to her when she passed on horseback that she was sure she would want her to come. The French peasants love to be spoken to, always answer civilly, and are interested in the horses, or the donkey, or the children—anything that passes.

They were all streaming up the slippery hillside.

We couldn't loiter, as the bell was tolling, the children already at the church, and some one rushed down to say that "M. le Curé attendait ces dames pour commencer son office." There was quite a crowd on the little "place," everybody waiting for us to come in. We let the children troop in first, sitting on benches on one side. In front of the altar there were rows of chairs for the "quality." The Sisters and their girls sat close up to the harmonium, and on a table near, covered with a pretty white linen cloth trimmed with fine old lace (part of the church property), was the Enfant Jésus in his cradle. This was to be a great surprise to me. When it was decided that the Sisters should come to the fête with some of the bigger girls, and bring the Enfant Jésus, they thought there must be a new dress for the "babe," so every child subscribed a sou, and the dress was made by the couturière of La Ferté. It *was* a surprise, for the Enfant Jésus was attired in a pink satin garment with the high puffed fashionable sleeves we were all wearing! However, I concealed my feelings, the good Sisters were so naïvely pleased. I could only hope the children would think the sleeves were wings.

As soon as the party from the château was seated, every one crowded in, and there were not seats enough, nor room enough in the little church; so the big doors remained open (it was fairly warm with the lights and the people), and there were nearly as many people outside as in. The three keepers (Garde de Borny and our two) looked very imposing. They are all big men, and their belts and gun-barrels bright and shining. They stood at the doors to keep order. The Mayor, too, was there, in a black coat and white cravat, but he came up to the top of the church and sat in the same row with me. He didn't have on his tricoloured scarf, so I suppose he doesn't possess one.

It was a pretty, simple service. When the curé and his two choir children in their short, white surplices and red petticoats came up the aisle, the choir sang the fine old hymn "Adeste Fideles," the congregation all joining in. We sang, too, the English words ("Oh, come, all ye Faithful"); we didn't know the Latin ones, but hoped nobody would notice. There were one or two prayers and a pretty, short address, talking of the wonderful Christmas night so many years ago, when the bright star guided the shepherds through the cold winter night to the stable where the heavenly babe was born. The children listened most attentively, and as all the boys in the village begin life as shepherds and cow-boys, they were wildly interested. Then there was a benediction, and at the end all the children in procession passed before the Enfant Jésus and kissed his foot. It was pretty to see the little ones standing up on tip-toe to get to the little foot, and the mothers holding up their babes. While this was going on, the choir sang the Noël Breton of Holmès, "Deux anges sont venus ce soir m'apporter de bien belles choses." There was some little delay in getting the children into procession again to go down to the school-house. They had been supernaturally good, but were so impatient to see the Tree that it was difficult to hold them. Henrietta and Pauline hurried on to light the Tree. I waited for the Abbé. He was much pleased with the attendance, and spoke so nicely to all the people.

We found the children all assembled in the small room at the school-house, and as soon as we could get through the crowd we let them come in. The Tree was quite beautiful, all white candles—quantities—shiny ornaments and small toys, dolls, trumpets, drums, and the yellow and red bags of "dragées" hanging on the branches. It went straight up to the ceiling, and quite on top was a big gold star, the manufacture of which had been a source of great tribulation at the château. We forgot to get one in Paris, and sent in hot haste on Wednesday to La Ferté for pasteboard and gold paper; but, alas! none of us could draw, and we had no model. I made one or two attempts, with anything but a satisfactory result: all the points were of different lengths and there was nothing but points (more like an octopus than anything else). However, Pauline finally produced a very good one (it really looked like a star), and of course the covering it with gold paper was easy. The crèche made a great effect, standing at the bottom of the Tree with a tall candle on each side. All the big toys and clothes were put on a table behind, where we all sat. Then the door was opened; there was a rush at first, but the school-mistress kept strict order. The little ones came first, their eyes round and fixed on the beautiful Tree; then the bigger children, and immediately behind them the "oldest inhabitants"—such a collection of old, bent, wrinkled, crippled creatures—then as many as could get in. There wasn't a sound at first, except some very small babies crowing and choking—then a sort of hum of pleasure.

We had two or three recitations in parts from the older scholars; some songs, and at the end the "compliment," the usual thing—"Madame et chère Bienfaitrice," said by a small thing about five years old, speaking very fast and low, trying to look at me, but turning her head always toward the Tree and being shaken back into her place by Madame Isidore. Then we began the distribution—the clothes first, so as not to despoil the Tree too soon. The children naturally didn't take the slightest interest in warm petticoats or tricots, but their mothers did.

We had the little ones first, Francis giving to the girls and Alice to the boys. Henrietta called the names; Pauline gave the toys to our two, and Madame Isidore called up each child. The faces of the children, when they saw dolls, trumpets, etc., being taken off the Tree and handed to each of them, was a thing to remember. The little girls with their dolls were too sweet, hugging them tight in their little fat arms. One or two of the boys began to blow softly on the trumpets and beat the drums, and were instantly hushed up by the parents; but we said they might make as much noise as they pleased for a few moments, and a fine "vacarme" (row) it was—the heavy boots of the boys contributing well as they moved about after their trains, marbles, etc.

However, the candles were burning low (they only just last an hour) and we thought it was time for cakes and wine. We asked the children if they were pleased, also if each child had garment, toy, and "dragées," and to hold them up. There was a great scamper to the mothers to get the clothes, and then all the arms went up with their precious load.

The school-children passed first into the outer room, where the keepers' wives and our maids were presiding over two great bowls of hot wine (with a great deal of water, naturally) and a large tray filled with brioches. When each child had had a drink and a cake they went out, to make room for the outsiders and old people. Henrietta and Pauline distributed the "extras"; I think there were about twenty in all, counting the babies in arms—also, of course, the girls from La Ferté who had come over with the Sisters to sing. I talked to some of the old people. There was one poor old woman—looked a hundred—still gazing spellbound at the Tree with the candles dying out, and most of the ornaments taken off. As I came up to her she said: "Je suis bien vieille, mais je n'aurais jamais cru voir quelque chose de si beau! Il me semble que le ciel est ouvert"—poor old thing! I am so glad I wasn't sensible, and decided to give them something pretty to look at and think about. There was wine and cakes for all, and then came the closing ceremony.

We (the quality) adjourned to the sitting-room of the school-mistress (where there were red arm-chairs and a piano), who produced a bottle of better wine, and then we "trinquéd" (touched glasses) with the Mayor, who thanked us in the name of the commune for the beautiful fête we had made for them. I answered briefly that I was quite happy to see them so happy, and then we all made a rush for wraps and carriages.

All the children in procession passed.

There was some poor old woman still gazing spellbound.

The Abbé came back to the château to dine, but he couldn't get away until he had seen his Sisters and harmonium packed safely into the big omnibus and started for La Ferté. It looked so pretty all the way home. It was quite dark, and the various groups were struggling down the hill and along the road, their lanterns making a bright spot on the snow; the little childish voices talking, laughing, and little bands running backward and forward, some disappearing at a turn of the road, the lantern getting dimmer, and finally vanishing behind the trees. We went very slowly, as the roads were dreadfully slippery, and had a running escort all the way to the Mill of Bourneville, with an accompaniment of drums and trumpets. The melancholy plains of the Valois were transformed tonight. In every direction we saw little twinkling lights, as the various bands separated and struck off across the fields to some lonely farm or mill. It is a lonely, desolate country—all great stretches of fields and plains, with a far-away blue line of forests. We often drive for miles without meeting a vehicle of any kind, and there are such distances between the little hamlets and isolated farms that one is almost uncomfortable in the absolute solitude. In winter no one is working in the fields and one never hears a sound; a dog's bark is welcome—it means life and movement somewhere.

It is quite the country of the "haute culture," which Cherbuliez wrote about in his famous novel, "La Ferme du Choquart." The farms are often most picturesque—have been "abbayes" and monasteries. The massive round towers, great gate-ways, and arched windows still remain; occasionally, too, parts of a solid wall. There is a fine old ruin—the "Commanderie," near Montigny, one of our poor little villages. It belonged to the Knights Templars, and is most interesting. The chapel walls are still intact, and the beautiful roof and high, narrow windows. It is now, alas! a "poulailler" (chicken-house), and turkeys and chickens are perched on the rafters and great beams that still support the roof. The dwelling-house, too, is most interesting with its thick gray walls, high narrow windows, and steep winding staircase. I was always told there were "donjons" in the cellars, but I never had the courage to go down the dark, damp, slippery staircase.

We were quite glad to get back to our big drawing-room with the fire and the tea-table; for of course the drawback to our entertainment was the stuffiness (not to say bad smell) of the little room. When all the children and grown people got in—most of them with damp clothes and shoes—the odour was something awful. Of course no window could be opened on account of the candles, and the atmosphere was terrible. At the end, when it was complicated with wine and cake and all the little ones' faces smeared with chocolate and "dragées," I really don't know how we stood it.

We had a very cheerful dinner. We complimented the Abbé upon his sermon, which was really very pretty and poetical. He said the children's faces quite inspired him, and beyond, over their heads, through the open door he got a glimpse of the tall pines with their frosted heads, and could almost fancy he saw the beautiful star.

We were all much pleased with our first "Christmas in the Valois."

VII

A RACINE CELEBRATION

MAREUIL-SUR-OURCQ, April 20th, 1899.

I could scarcely believe I was in our quiet little town of La Ferté-Milon to-day. Such a transformation—flags flying, draperies at all the windows, garlands of greens and flowers across the streets, and a fine triumphal arch—all greens and flowers arranged about the centre of the Grande Rue. Many people standing about, looking on, and making suggestions; altogether, an air de fête which is most unusual in these sleepy little streets where nothing ever passes, except at four o'clock, when the three schools come out, and clatter down the street. The École Maternelle comes first, the good Mère Cécile bringing up the rear of the procession, holding the smallest children, babies three and four years old, by the hand, three or four more clinging to her skirts, and guiding them across the perilous passage of the bridge over the canal. It is a pretty view from the bridge. The canal (really the river Ourcq, canalisée), which has preserved its current and hasn't the dead, sluggish look of most canals, runs alongside of the Mail, a large green place with grass, big trees, a broad walk down the centre, and benches under the trees. It is a sort of promenade for the inhabitants and also serves as a village green, where all the fairs, shows and markets are held. The opposite bank is bordered by quaint old houses, with round towers and gardens, full of bright flowers, running down to the water's edge. There is one curious old colombier which has been there for centuries; near the bridge there is a lavoir, where there are always women washing. They are all there to-day, but much distracted, wildly interested in all that is going on—and the unwonted stir in the streets; chattering hard, and giving their opinions as to the decoration of the arch, which is evidently a source of great pride to the town.

On a bright sunny day, when the red roofs and flowers are reflected in the water, and it is not too cold, their work doesn't seem very hard; but on a winter afternoon, when they have to break the ice sometimes, and a biting wind is blowing down the canal, it is pitiable to see the poor things thinly clad, shivering and damp; their hands and arms red and chapped with cold. On the other side of the bridge, the canal wanders peacefully along through endless green meadows, bordered with poplars, to Marolles, a little village where there is the first écluse on the way to Paris.

We had been talking vaguely all winter of doing something at La Ferté-Milon to fêter the bicentenaire of Racine. They were making preparations at Paris, also at

Port Royal, and it seemed hard to do nothing in his native place. His statue in the Grande Rue is one of the glories of La Ferté.

Jean Racine was born in La Ferté in 1639. He lost both father and mother young, and was brought up by his grandparents. He was sent first to school at Beauvais, later, while still quite a youth, to Port Royal. His stay there influenced considerably his character and his writings; and though he separated himself entirely from the "Solitaires" during the years of his brilliant career as poet and courtier, there remained always in his heart a latent tenderness for the quiet green valley of the Chevreuse, where he had passed all his years of adolescence, listening to the good Fathers, and imbibing their doctrines of the necessity of divine grace to complete the character. His masters were horrified and distressed when his talent developed into plays, which brought him into contact with actors and actresses, and made him an habitué of a frivolous Court.

There is a pretty letter from one of his aunts, a religieuse de Port Royal, begging him to keep away from "des fréquentations abominables," and to return to a Christian life.

His career was rapid and brilliant. He was named to the Académie Française in 1673, and when he retired from the theatre was a welcome and honoured guest at the most brilliant court of the world. He was made private historian to the King and accompanied him on various campaigns. There are amusing mentions of the poets-historians (Boileau was also royal historian) in the writings of their contemporaries, "les messieurs du sublime," much embarrassed with their military accoutrements and much fatigued by the unwonted exercise and long days on horseback. The King showed Racine every favour. He was lodged at Versailles and at Marly and was called upon to amuse and distract the monarch when the cares of state and increasing years made all diversions pall upon him. He saw the decline and disgrace of Madame de Montespan, the marvellous good fortune of Madame de Maintenon. His famous tragedies of Esther and Athalie were written at Madame de Maintenon's request for her special institution of St. Cyr, and the performances were honoured by the presence of the King. Racine himself directed the rehearsals and the music was composed by Jean Baptiste Moreau, organist of St. Cyr. The youthful actresses showed wonderful aptitude in interpreting the passionate, tender verses of the poet. Young imaginations worked and jealousies and rivalries ran high. After a certain number of representations Mme. de Maintenon was obliged to suspend the performances in public, with costumes and music. The plays were only given in private at the Maison de St. Cyr; the young scholars playing in the dress of the establishment. He made his peace with Port Royal before he died. He submitted Phèdre to his former masters and had the satisfaction of being received again by the "Grand Arnauld,"[10] who had been deeply offended by his ingratitude and his criticisms and ridicule of many of his early friends and protec-

[10] "Le Grand Arnauld" (Antoine), one of the first and most influential of the celebrated "Solitaires" who established themselves at Port Royal, and one of the founders of the famous sect of Jansenists whose controversies with the Jesuits convulsed the whole religious world in France during the years 1662-1668. He was followed in his retreat by his mother (after the husband's death), his brother and four sisters, one of whom became the "Mère Angélique," Abbesse of Port Royal.

tors. He asked to be buried there, and his body remained until the destruction and devastation of Port Royal, when it was removed to Paris and placed in the Church of St. Etienne des Monts.

He returned many times to La Ferté-Milon, and the great poet and private historian of the Roi Soleil must often have climbed the steep little street that leads to the ruins, and thought of the changes, since the little boy lay on the grass at the foot of the great walls, dreaming golden dreams of the future, which for him were so brilliantly realised.

In a small country town one is slow to adopt new ideas, slower still to carry them out, but the Mayor and curé were both most anxious to do something in the birthplace of the poet, and that was the general feeling in the Department. After many discussions we finally arrived at a solution, or at least we decided what we wanted: a special service in the fine old church of Notre Dame, which stands beautifully on the hill, close to the ruins; a representation of the Comédie Française, and of course a banquet at the Sauvage, with all the official world, senators, Préfet, Académiciens—a band of music, a torchlight procession, and as many distinguished visitors as we could get hold of. *Funds* of course were a necessary item, but all the countryside contributed largely, and we knew that the artists would give their services gratis.

We arranged a breakfast at my house in Paris with Mons. Casimir-Périer, late President of the Republic, who was always ready to lend his influence for anything that interests the people, and teaches them something of their great men, and Mons. Claretie, Directeur of the Comédie Française, a most cultivated, charming man. He is generally rather chary of letting his pensionnaires play en province, but this really was an occasion to break through his rules, and he was quite ready to help us in every way. We had also M. Sebline, Senator of the Aisne, and l'Abbé Maréchal, curé of La Ferté-Milon. We had wanted one of the Administrateurs of the Chemin de Fer du Nord to arrange about a free transport for the actors, but there seemed some trouble about getting hold of the right man, and Sebline promised to see about that.

The Abbe Maréchal and I were very ambitious for the theatrical part of the entertainment and had views of Esther with the costumes, and choruses of Moreau, but M. Claretie said that would be impossible. It was difficult enough to arrange in Paris with all the singers, instruments, and costumes at hand—and would be impossible in the country with our modest resources. I think the idea of a tent on a village green rather frightened him; and he didn't quite see the élite of his company playing in such a cadre—no décor—and probably very bad acoustics. However, Sebline reassured him. He knew the tent and its capabilities, having seen it figure on various occasions, comices agricoles, banquets de pompiers, at village fêtes generally, and said it could be arranged quite well.

We discussed many programmes, but finally accepted whatever M. Claretie would give—an act of "Les Plaideurs," and two or three of "Bérénice," with Mme. Bartet, who is charming in that rôle. The Abbé Maréchal undertook the music in his church, and I was sure he would succeed in having some of the choruses of

Esther. His heart was quite set on it. Once he had settled our programme, the conversation drifted away from the purely local talk, and was brilliant enough. All the men were clever and good talkers, and all well up in Racine, his career, and the various phases of his work.

From the classics we got into modern plays and poets, and there of course the differences of opinion were wide; but I think the general public (people in the upper galleries) like better when they go to the Française to see a classic piece—Roman emperors and soldiers, and vestal virgins and barbarians in chains—and to listen to their long tirades. The modern light comedy, even when it treats of the vital subjects of the day, seems less in its place in those old walls. I quite understand one couldn't see Britannicus,[11] Mithridate, nor the Cid every evening.

We came down here several times to see how things were getting on, and always found the little town quite feverishly animated. We had succeeded in getting the band of the regiment stationed at Soissons. I wrote to the Colonel, who said he would send it with pleasure, but that he couldn't on his own authority. An application must be made to the Ministère de la Guerre. There is always so much red tape in France. One writes and receives so many letters about anything one wants to do—a Christmas Tree in the school-house—a distribution of soup for the poor and old—a turn in a road to be rounded, etc. However, the permission was graciously accorded for the band. The Mayor's idea was to station it on the Mail, where quantities of people would congregate who couldn't get into the church or the tent.

We went one day to have tea with the Abbé Maréchal in his nice old presbytère; the salon opening out on a large, old-fashioned garden with fine trees, and a view of the church towers in the distance. He was quite pleased with all that he had arranged for his church service. One of his friends, Abbé Vignon, a most interesting man and eloquent preacher, promised to deliver a lecture on Racine from the pulpit; and M. Vincent d'Indy, the distinguished composer and leader of the modern school of music, undertook the music with Mme. Jeanne Maunay as singer; he himself presiding at the organ.

I tried to persuade the proprietors of all the châteaux in the neighbourhood to come, but I can't say I had much success. Some had gout—some had mourning. I don't remember if any one "had married a wife and therefore couldn't come."

However, we shall fill our own house, and give breakfast and dinner to any one who will come. To-day we have been wandering about on the green near the ruins, trying to find some place where we can give our friends tea. The service in the church will certainly be long, and before the theatrical performance begins we should like to arrange a little goûter—but where? It is too far to go back to our

[11] I remember so well our cousin Arthur's description of his holidays spent at his grandmother's château. Every evening they read aloud some classical piece. When he had read Britannicus twice (the second time to appreciate more fully the beauties which were lightly passed over at first), he rebelled, had a migraine, or a sore throat, something which prevented his appearing in the drawing-room after dinner; and he and his cousins attired themselves in sheets, and stood on the corner of the wall where the diligence made a sharp turn, frightening the driver and his horses out of their wits.

house, and the Sauvage, our usual resort, will be packed on that day, and quite off its head, as they have two banquets morning and evening. The "Cafe des Ruines," a dirty little place just under the great walls of the château, didn't look inviting; but there was literally nothing else, so we interviewed the proprietor, went in to the big room down stairs, which was perfectly impossible, reeking with smoke, and smelling of cheap liquor; but he told us he had a "très belle salle" up stairs, where we should be quite alone. We climbed up a dark, rickety little turning staircase, and found ourselves in quite a good room, with three large windows on the green; the walls covered with pictures from the cheap illustrated papers, and on the whole not too dirty. We have taken it for the afternoon, told the patron we would come to-morrow, put up tables, and make as many preparations as we could for the great day. He was very anxious to furnish something—some "vin du pays;" but we told him all we wanted was fire, plenty of hot water, and a good scrubbing of floor and windows.

It is enchanting this afternoon. We are taking advantage of the fine weather to drive about the country, and show our friends some of our big farms and quaint little villages. They look exactly as they did a hundred years ago, "when the Cossacks were here," as they say in the country. Some of the inns have still kept their old-fashioned signs and names. Near May, on the road to Meaux, Bossuet's fine old cathedral town, there is a nice old square red-brick house, "L'Auberge du Veau qui Téte" (The Inn of the Sucking Calf), which certainly indicates that this is great farming country. There are quantities of big white oxen, cows, and horses in the fields, but the roads are solitary. One never meets anything except on market day. The Florians who live in Seine et Marne, which is thickly populated—villages and châteaux close together—were much struck with the loneliness and great stretches of wood and plain.

We are praying for fine weather, as rain would be disastrous. The main street looks really charming. The green arch is nearly finished, and at night, when everything is illuminated, will be most effective.

22nd. It rained yesterday afternoon and all night—not light April showers, but a good, steady downpour. Francis and Ctesse. de Gontaut arrived from Paris in his little open automobile. Such a limp, draggled female as emerged from the little carriage I never saw. They had had some sharp showers; pannes (breakdowns), too, and she *says* she pushed the carriage up all the hills. She didn't seem either tired or cross, and looked quite bright and rested when she reappeared at dinner.

Various friends arrived this morning, and we have been in La Ferté all the afternoon. The draperies and festoons of flowers don't look any the worse for the heavy rain, and at least it is over, and we shall probably have sun to-morrow. The tent is up on the green, and looks fairly large. I don't think any one will see anything except in the first eight or ten rows of chairs, but it seems they will all hear. The stage was being arranged, and, much to our amusement, they told us the Empire chairs and tables had been lent by the Abbé Maréchal. He is a collectionneur, and has some handsome furniture. We inspected our tea-room, which didn't look too bad. Our men were there with tables, china, etc., and when it is all arranged we shall have quite a respectable buffet. The landlord was very anxious to decorate the tables with greens, flags, and perhaps a bust of Racine with a crown of laurels, but we told him it would be better not to complicate things.

The view was lovely to-day from the top of the hill—the ruins looking enormous, standing out against the bright blue sky, and soft and pink at the top where the outline was irregular and the walls crumbling a little. We had some difficulty in collecting our party, and finally discovered Francis, Ctesse de Gontaut and Christiani having chocolate and cakes in the back parlour of the grocer's shop (nothing like equality on these occasions), who was telling them all the little gossip of the town, and naming the radicals who wouldn't go to the church.

We had a pleasant evening with music and "baraque"—which is not very fatiguing as a mental exercise. I tried to send all the party to bed early, and have come upstairs myself, but I still hear the click of the billiard balls, and sounds of merriment downstairs. It is a splendid starlight night, the sky quite blue over the pines. I think we shall have beautiful weather for our fête. I have very vague ideas as to how many people we shall have for breakfast and dinner to-morrow, but the "office" is warned. I hope we shan't starve.

April 24th. Monday.

We had a beautiful and most successful day yesterday. All the household was stirring fairly early, as we had to get ourselves in to La Ferté before 12 o'clock. We started in all sorts of conveyances—train, carriage, voiturette—and found the Grande Rue full of people. The official breakfast was over, also the visit to the Mairie, where there are a few souvenirs of the poet—his picture, acte de naissance,[12] and signature. The procession was just forming to climb up the steep, little street that leads to the church, so we took a short cut (still steeper), and waited outside the doors to see them arrive. It was a pretty sight to see the cortège wind up the path—the Bishop of Soissons and several other ecclesiastics in their robes, blackcoated officials, some uniforms—the whole escorted by groups of children running alongside, and a fair sprinkling of women in light dresses, with flowers on their hats, making patches of colour. The church was crowded—one didn't remark the absence of certain "esprits forts" who gloried in remaining outside—and the service was most interesting. The lecture or rather "Éloge de Racine" was beautifully given by the Abbé Vignot. It was not very easy for a priest to pronounce from the pulpit an eulogium on the poet and dramatic author who had strayed so far from the paths of grace and the early teachings of Port Royal, where the "petit Racine" had been looked upon as a model pupil destined to rise high in the ecclesiastical world; but the orator made us see through the sombre tragedies of Phèdre, Britannicus and others the fine nature of the poet, who understood so humanly the passions that tempt and warp the soul, and showed a spirit of tolerance very remarkable in those days. He dwelt less upon the courtier; spoke more of the Christian of his last days. He certainly lent to the "charm of the poet, the beauty of his voice," for it was impossible to hear anything more perfect than the intonation

[12] Birth certificate.

and diction of the speaker.

There was a short address from Monseigneur Deramecourt, Bishop of Soissons—a stately figure seated on the Episcopal throne in the chancel. The music was quite beautiful. We had the famous "Chanteurs de St. Gervais," and part of the chœurs d'Esther, composed by Moreau, and sung in splendid style by Mme. Jeanne Maunay, M. Vincent d'Indy accompanying on the organ. The simple sixteenth century chaunts sung by the St. Gervais choir sounded splendidly in the fine old cathedral. The tones seemed fuller and richer than in their Paris church.

We went out a little before the end to see what was going on on the green. It was still quite a climb from the church, and all the people of the upper town had turned out to see the sight. It is quite a distinct population from the lower town. They are all canal hands, and mostly a very bad lot. The men generally drink—not enough to be really intoxicated (one rarely sees that in France), but enough to make them quarrelsome; and the women almost all slatternly and idle. They were standing at their doors, babies in their arms, and troops of dirty, ragged, pretty little children playing on the road, and accompanying us to the green, begging for "un petit sou."

We saw the cortège winding down again, the robes and banners of the clergy making a great effect, and we heard in the distance the strains of the military band stationed on the Mail—echoes of the Marseillaise and the "Père la Victoire" making a curious contrast to the old-world music we had just been listening to in the church. Our party scattered a little. Francis went down to the station with his auto to get the Duc and Duchesse d'Albufera, who had promised to come for the Comédie and dinner. They are neighbours, and have a beautiful place not very far off—Montgobert, in the heart of the Villers-Cotteret forest. He is a descendant of Suchet, one of Napoleon's Marshals, and they have a fine picture of the Marshal in uniform, and various souvenirs of the Emperor. Francis had some difficulty in making his way through the Grande Rue which was packed with people very unwilling to let any vehicle pass. However, they had a certain curiosity about the little carriage, which is the first one to appear in this part of the country—where one sees only farmers' gigs on two high wheels, or a tapissière, a covered carriage for one horse. However, as every one knew him they were good natured enough, and let him pass, but he could not get any further than the foot of the street—too steep for any carriage to venture.

It was a pretty sight as we got to the Place. Quantities of people walking about—many evident strangers, seeing the ruins for the first time. There was a band of schoolboys, about twenty, with a priest, much excited. They wanted to go in the tent and get good places, but were afraid of missing something outside, and were making little excursions in every direction, evidently rather worrying their Director. The tent, fairly large, looked small under the shadow of the great walls. We looked in and found a good many people already in their places, and saw that the first two or three rows of red arm-chairs were being kept for the quality. One of the sights was our two tall men standing at the door of the rather dirty, dilapidated "Cafe des Ruines," piloting our friends past the groups of workmen smoking and drinking in the porch, and up the dark, rickety staircase. I don't think any one would have had the courage to go up, if Henrietta hadn't led the way—once up, the effect of our banqueting-hall was not bad. The servants had made it look very well with china and silver brought from the house, also three or four fresh pictures taken from the illustrated papers to cover those which already existed, and which looked rather the worse for smoke and damp. We were actually obliged to cover General Boulanger and his famous black charger with a "Bois de Boulogne le Matin," with carriages, riders, bicycles, pretty women and children strolling about.

The view from the windows was charming, and it was amusing to watch all the people toiling up the path. We recognised many friends, and made frantic signs to them to come and have tea. We had about three-quarters of an hour before the Comédie began, and when we got to the tent it was crowded—all the dignitaries—Bishop, Préfet, Senator, Deputy (he didn't object to the theatrical performance), M. Henri Houssaye, Académician; M. Roujon, Directeur des Beaux Arts, sitting in the front row in their red arm-chairs, and making quite as much of a show for the villagers as the actors.

The performance began with the third act of "Les Plaideurs," played with extraordinary entrain. There were roars of laughter all through the salle, or tent—none more amused than the band of schoolboys, and their youthful enjoyment was quite contagious. People turned to look at them, and it was evident that, if they didn't see, they *heard,* as they never missed a point—probably knew it all by heart. Then came a recitation by Mlle. Moreno, who looked and spoke like a tragic muse the remorse and suffering of Phèdre. The end of the performance—the two last acts of Bérénice—was enchanting. Mme. Bartet looked charming in her floating blue draperies, and was the incarnation of the resigned, poetic, loving woman; Paul Mounet was a grand, sombre, passionate Titus, torn between his love for the beautiful Queen and his duty as a Roman to choose only one of his own people to share his throne and honours. The Roman Senate was an all-powerful body, and a woman's love too slight a thing to oppose to it. Bartet was charming all through, either in her long plaintes to her Confidante, where one felt that in spite of her repeated assurances of her lover's tenderness there was always the doubt of the Emperor's faith or in her interviews with Titus—reproaching him and adoring him, with all the magic of her voice and smile. It was a triumph for them both, and their splendid talent. With no décor, no room, no scenic illusions of any kind, they held their audience enthralled. No one minded the heat, nor the crowd, nor the uncomfortable seats, and all were sorry when the well-known lines, said by Mme. Bartet, in her beautiful, clear, pathetic voice

> "Servons tous trois d'exemple à l'Univers
> De l'amour la plus tendre et la plus malheureuse
> Dont il puisse garder l'histoire douloureuse,"

brought to a close the fierce struggle between love and ambition.

As soon as it was over, I went with Sebline to compliment the actors. We found Bartet, not in her dressing-room, but standing outside, still in her costume, very busy photographing Mounet, superb as a Roman Emperor. He was posing most impatiently, watching the sun slowly sinking behind the ruins, as he wanted to photograph Bérénice before the light failed, and the time was short. They were surrounded by an admiring crowd, the children much interested in the "beautiful lady with the stars all over her dress." We waited a few moments, and had a little talk with them. They said the fête had interested them very much and they were very glad to have come. They were rather taken aback at first when they saw the tent, the low small stage, and the very elementary scenery—were afraid the want of space would bother them, but they soon felt that they held their audience, and that their voices carried perfectly. They were rather hurried, as they were all taking the train back to Paris, except Bartet, who had promised to stay for the banquet. I had half hoped she would come to me, but of course I was obliged to waive my claim. When I saw how much the Préfet and the official world held to having her—when I heard afterwards that she had had the seat of honour next to the Bishop I was very glad I hadn't insisted, as she certainly doesn't often have the opportunity of sitting next to a Bishop. It seems he was delighted with her.

We loitered about some little time, talking to all our friends. The view from the terrace was beautiful—directly at our feet the little town, which is literally two streets forming a long cross, the Grande Rue a streak of light and color, filled with people moving about, and the air alive with laughter and music. Just beyond, the long stretches of green pasture lands, cut every now and then by narrow lanes with apple trees and hawthorn in flower, and the canal winding along between the green walls of poplars—the whole hemmed in by the dark blue line of the Villers-Cotteret forest, which makes a grand sweep on the horizon.

It was lovely driving back to Mareuil, toward the bright sunset clouds. We had a gay dinner and evening. I never dared ask where the various men dressed who came to dinner. The house is not very large, and every room was occupied—but as they all appeared most correctly attired, I suppose there are resources in the way of lingerie and fumoir which are available at such times, and Francis's valet de chambre is so accustomed to having more people than the house can hold that he probably took his precautions. Francis started off for the banquet at the Sauvage in his voiturette, but that long-suffering vehicle having made hundreds of kilomètres these last days, came to grief at the foot of "la Montagne de Marolles," and he was towed back by a friendly carter and arrived much disgusted when we were half through dinner.

We heard all the details of the dinner from the Abbé Maréchal. Certainly the banqueting hall of the Sauvage will not soon again see such a brilliant assembly. Madame Bartet was the Queen of the Fête, and sat between the Bishop and the Préfet. There were some pretty speeches from M. Henri Houssaye, M. Roujon—and of course the toast of the President accompanied by the Marseillaise.

The departure to the train was most amusing—all the swells, including Bartet, walking in the cortége, escorted by a torch-light procession, and surrounded by the entire population of La Ferté.

The Grande Rue was illuminated from one end to the other, red Bengal lights throwing out splendidly the grand old château and the towers of Notre Dame.

VIII

A CORNER OF NORMANDY

BAGNOLES DE L'ORNE, July-August.

It is lovely looking out of my window this morning, so green and cool and quiet. I had my petit déjeuner on my balcony, a big tree in the garden making perfect shade and a wealth of green wood and meadow in every direction, so resting to the eyes after the Paris asphalt. It seems a very quiet little place. Scarcely anything passing—a big omnibus going, I suppose, to the baths, and a butcher's cart. For the last ten minutes I have been watching a nice-looking sunburned girl with a big straw hat tied down over her ears, who is vainly endeavouring to get her small donkey-cart, piled high with fruit and vegetables, up a slight incline to the gate of a villa just opposite. She has been struggling for some time, pulling, talking, and red with the exertion. One or two workmen have come to her assistance, but they can't do anything either. The donkey's mind is made up. There is an animated conversation—I am too high up to hear what they say. Finally she leaves her cart, ties up her fruit in her apron, balances a basket of eggs with one hand on her head, and disappears into the garden behind the gate. No one comes along and the cart is quite unmolested. I think I should have gone down myself if I had seen anyone making off with any of the fruit. It is a delightful change from the hot stuffy August Paris I left yesterday. My street is absolutely deserted, every house closed except mine, the sun shining down hard on the white pavement, and perfect stillness all day. The evenings from seven till ten are indescribable—a horror of musical concierges with accordions, a favorite French instrument. They all sit outside their doors with their families and friends, playing and singing all the popular songs, and at intervals all joining in a loud chorus of "Viens Poupoule." Grooms are teaching lady friends to ride bicycles, a lot of barking, yapping fox-terriers running alongside. There is a lively cross-conversation going on from one side of the street to the other, my own concierge and chauffeur contributing largely. Of course my balcony is untenable, and I am obliged to sit inside, until happily sleep descends upon them. They all vanish, and the street relapses into perfect silence. I am delighted to find myself in this quiet little Norman bathing-place, just getting known to the French and foreign public.

It is hardly a village; the collection of villas, small houses, shops, and two enormous hotels surrounding the établissement seems to have sprung up quite suddenly and casually in the midst of the green fields and woods, shut in on all sides almost by the Forest of Ardennes, which makes a beautiful curtain of verdure. There are villas dotted about everywhere, of every possible style; Norman chalets, white and gray, with the black crossbeams that one is so familiar with all over this part of the country; English cottages with verandas and bow-windows; three or four rather pretentious looking buildings with high perrons and one or two terraces; gardens with no very pretty flowers, principally red geraniums, some standing back in a nice little green wood, some directly on the road with benches along the fence so that the inhabitants can see the passers-by (and get all the dust of the roads). But there isn't much passing even in these days of automobiles. There are two trains from Paris, arriving at two in the afternoon and at eleven at night. The run down from Paris, especially after Dreux, is charming, almost like driving through a park. The meadows are beautifully green and the trees very fine—the whole country very like England in appearance, recalling it all the time, particularly when we saw pretty gray old farm-houses in the distance—and every now and then a fine Norman steeple.

There are two rival hotels and various small pensions and family houses. We are staying at the Grand, which is very comfortable. There is a splendid terrace overlooking the lake; rather an ambitious name for the big pond, which does, however, add to the picturesqueness of the place, particularly at night, when all the lights are reflected in the water. The whole hotel adjourns there after dinner, and people walk up and down and listen to the music until ten o'clock. After that there is a decided falling off of the beau monde. Many people take their bath at half past five in the morning and are quite ready to go to bed early. The walk down in the early morning is charming, through a broad, shaded alley—Allée de Dante. I wonder why it is called that. I don't suppose the poet ever took warm baths or douches in any description of établissement. I remember the tale we were always told when we were children, and rebelled against the perpetual cleansing and washing that went on in the nursery, of the Italian countess who said she would be ashamed, if she couldn't do all her washing in a glass of water. It is rather amusing to see all the types. I don't think there are many foreigners. I hear very little English spoken, though they tell me there are some English here. We certainly don't look our best in the early morning, but the women stand the test better than the men. With big hats, veils, and the long cloaks they wear now, they pass muster very well and don't really look any worse than when they are attired for a spin in an open auto; but the men, with no waistcoats, a foulard around their throats, and a very dejected air, don't have at all the conquering-hero appearance that one likes to see in the stronger sex.

The établissement is large and fairly good, but nothing like what one finds in all the Austrian and German baths. When I first go in, coming out of the fresh morning air, I am rather oppressed with the smell of hot air, damp clothing, and many people crowded into little hot bath-rooms. There are terrible little dark closets called cabinets de repos. Many doctors in white waistcoats and red ribbons are walking about; plenty of baigneuses, with their sleeves rolled up, showing a red arm that evidently has been constantly in the water; people who have had their baths and are resting, wrapped up in blankets, stretched out on long chairs near the windows; bells going all the time, cries of "Marie-Louise," "Jeanne," "Anne-Marie." It is rather a pandemonium. Our baigneuse, who is called Marie-Louise, is upstairs. At the top of the stairs there is a grand picture of the horse who discovered the Bagnoles waters, a beautiful white beast standing in a spring, all water lilies and sparkling water. A lovely young lady in a transparent green garment with roses over each ear, like the head-dress one sees on Japanese women, is holding his bridle. The legend says that a certain gallant and amorous knight of yore, having become old and crippled with rheumatism, and unable any longer to make a brave show in tournaments under fair ladies' eyes, determined to retire from the world, and to leave his horse—faithful companion of many jousts—in a certain green meadow traversed by a babbling brook, where he could end his days in peace. What was his surprise, some months later, to find his horse quietly standing again in his old stable, his legs firm and straight, his skin glossy, quite renovated. The master took himself off to the meadow, investigated the quality of the water, bathed himself, and began life anew with straightened limbs and quickened pulses. The waters certainly do wonders. We see every day people who had arrived on crutches or walking with canes quite discarding them after a course of baths.

The hotel is full, mostly French, but there are of course some exceptions. We have a tall and stately royal princess with two daughters and a niece. The girls are charming—simple, pretty, and evidently much pleased to be away for a little while from court life and etiquette. They make their curé quite regularly, like any one else, walking and sitting in the Allée Dante. The people don't stare at them too much. There are one or two well-known men—deputies, membres de l'Institut—but, of course, women are in the majority. There is a band—not very good, as the performers, some of them good enough alone, had never played together until they came here. However, it isn't of much consequence, as no one listens. I make friends with them, as usual; something always draws me to artists. The boy at the piano looks so thin—really as if he did not get enough to eat. He plays very well, told me he was a premier prix of the Conservatoire de Madrid. When one thinks of the hours of work and fatigue that means, it is rather pathetic to see him, contented to earn a few francs a night, pounding away at a piano and generally ending with a "cake walk," danced by some enterprising young people with all sorts of remarkable steps and gestures, which would certainly astonish the original negro performers on a plantation.

The view from the terrace at night is pretty—quantities of lights twinkling about among the trees, and beyond, always on each side and in front, the thick green walls of the forest quite shutting in the quiet little place. We are usually the last outside. It grows cooler as the evening gets on, and I fancy it is not wise to sit out too late after the hot bath and fatigue of the day.

It is a splendid automobiling country, and every afternoon there is a goodly show of motors of all sizes and makes waiting to take their owners on some of the many interesting excursions which abound in this neighbourhood. We have an English friend who has brought over his automobile, a capital one—English make—and we have been out several times with him. The other day we went to Domfront—a lovely road, almost all the way through woods, the forest of Audaine with its fine old trees making splendid shade. We passed through the Étoile—well known to all the hunting men, as it is a favourite rendezvous de chasse. It is a lovely part of the forest, a great green space with alleys running off into the woods in all directions. Some of them, where the ground was a little hilly, looked like beautiful green paths going straight up to the clouds.

L'Etablissement, Bagnoles de l'Orme.

In Domfront some of the old towers are converted into modern dwellings.

We kept in the forest almost all the way—as we got near Domfront the road rising all the time, quite steep at the end, which, however, made no perceptible difference in our speed. The big auto galloped up all the hills quite smoothly and with no effort. It was a divine view as we finally emerged from the woods—miles of beautiful green meadows and hedges stretching away on each side and a blue line of hills in the distance. We had been told that we could see Mont St. Michel and the sea with our glasses, but we didn't, though the day was very clear. Domfront is a very old walled town, with round towers and a great square donjon, perched on the top of a mountain. A long stretch of solid wall is still there, and some of the old towers are converted into modern dwellings. It looked out of place to see ordinary lace curtains tied back with a ribbon and pots of red geraniums in the high narrow windows, when one thought of the rough grim soldiers armed to the teeth who have stood for hours in those same windows watching anxiously for the first glimpse of an armed band appearing at the edge of the meadows. The château must have been a fine feudal fortress in its time and has sheltered many great personages. William the Conqueror, of course—he has apparently lived in every château and sailed from every harbour in this part of Normandy—Charles IX, Catherine de Medicis, and the Montgomery who killed Henri II in tournament.

It was too early to go home, so we went on to the Château de Lassay. We raced through pretty little clean gray villages, looking peaceful and sleepy and deserted and evidently quite accustomed to automobiles. No one took much notice of us. There were only a few old people and children in the streets; all the men were working in the fields gathering in their harvest. Lassay is quite a place, with hotels, shops, churches, and an old Benedictine convent. We left the auto in the square, as it couldn't get up the narrow, steep little road to the hotel. There were swarms of beggars of all ages—old women, girls, children—lining the road before we got to the château. Monsieur B. (deputy), who was with us, remonstrated vigorously, particularly with stout, sturdy young women who were pursuing us, but they didn't care a bit, and we only got rid of them once we had crossed the moat and drawbridge and got into the court-yard, where a wrinkled and red-cheeked old woman locked the door after us. The château is almost entirely in ruins, but must have been splendid. There is a sort of modern dwelling-house in the inner court, but I fancy the proprietor rarely lives there. It is enormous. There are eight massive round towers connected by a courtine (little green path) that runs along the top of the ramparts. The big door that opens on the park is modern, and makes decidedly poor effect after the fine old pointed doorway that gives access to the great court-yard. The park, with a little care and a little money spent on it, would be beautiful, but it is quite wild and uncared for. There are splendid old trees, some of them covered entirely with ivy growing straight up into the branches and giving a most peculiar effect to the trees; ragged green paths leading to woods; running waters with little bridges thrown over them; a splendid vegetation everywhere, almost a jungle in some places—all utterly neglected. The old woman took us through the "casemates"—dark stone galleries with little narrow slits for windows or to fire through; they used to run all around the house, connected by a subterranean passage, but they are now, like all the rest, half in ruins. It was most interesting. We had not the energy, any of us, to go up into the tower and see the view—we had seen it all the way, culminating at Domfront on the top of the mountain, and though very beautiful, it is always the same—great stretches of green fields, hedges, and fine trees. It is a little too peaceful and monotonous for my taste. I like something bolder and wilder. A high granite cliff standing out in the sea, with the great Atlantic rollers breaking perpetually against it, appeals to me much more than green fields and cows standing placidly in little clear brooks, and clean, comfortable farmhouses, with pretty gray Norman steeples rising out of the woods, but my companions were certainly not of my opinion and were enchanted with the Norman landscape. We had a long ride back in the soft evening light. I am afraid to say how many kilomètres we went in the three hours we were away.

It has been warm these last days. There is a bit of road absolutely without shade of any kind we have to pass every time we go to the établissement, which is very trying. I love the early morning walk, everything is so fresh and the air singularly light and pure. It seems wicked to go into that atmosphere of hot air and suffering humanity, which greets one on the threshold of the bathhouse. To-day I have been driving with the princess. She does not like the automobile when she is making a cure—says it shakes her too much.

We had a pretty drive, past the château of Couterne, which is most picturesque. A beautiful beech avenue leads up to the house, which is built of brick, with round towers and a large pond or lake which comes right up to the walls. It is of the sixteenth century, and has been inhabited ever since by the same family. One of the ancestors was "chevalier et poète" of Queen Marguerite of Navarre. I had a nice talk with the princess about everything and everybody. I asked her if she had ever read "The Lightning Conductor." As her own auto is a Napier, I thought it would interest her. I told her all the potins (little gossip) of the hotel—that people said her youngest daughter was going to marry the King of Spain, and the general verdict was that the princess would make "a beautiful queen." Every one is horror-struck at the murder of the Russian Minister of the Interior, and I suppose it is only a beginning.

This afternoon I have been walking in the lovely woods at the back of the établissement. It is rather a steep climb to get to the point de vue and troublesome walking, as the paths are dry and slippery and the roots of the pine-trees that spread out over the paths catch one's heels sometimes. Some people spend all their day high up in the pines—take up books, seats, work, and goûter, and only come down after six, when the air gets cooler. We saw parties seated about in all directions and had glimpses of the white dresses, which are a uniform this year, flitting through the trees. It was very pretty, but not like the walls of Marienbad, with the splendid black pine forest all around and every now and then a glimpse of a green Alm (high field on the top of a mountain), with the peasant girl in her high Tyrolean hat and clean white chemisette standing on the edge, with her cows all behind her and the bells tinkling in the distance.

Château de Lassay.

It was so warm this evening that we sat out until ten o'clock. We had a visit from Comte de G., son-in-law of our friend Mrs. L.S. He lives at Deauville, and had announced himself for Monday morning for breakfast at twelve. He *did* come for breakfast, but on Tuesday morning, having been en route since Monday morning at seven o'clock. He was in an automobile and everything happened to him that can happen to an automobile except an absolute smash. He punctured his tires, had a big hole in his reservoir, his steering gear bent, his bougies always doing something they oughtn't to. He dined and slept at Falaise; rather a sketchy repast, but as he told us he could always get along with poached eggs, could eat six in an ordinary way and twelve in an emergency, we were reassured; for one can always get eggs and milk in Normandy. He arrived in a perfectly good humour and made himself very pleasant. He is an old soldier—a cavalry officer—and doesn't mind roughing it.

The journey from Deauville to Bagnoles is usually accomplished in three or four hours. Falaise, the birthplace of William the Conqueror, is an interesting old town, but looks as if it had been asleep ever since that great event. The old castle is very fine, stands high, close to the edge of the cliff, so that the rock seems to form part of the great walls. There is one fine round tower, and always the grass walk around the ramparts.

The views are beautiful. Looking down from one of the narrow, pointed windows, still fairly preserved, we had the classic Norman landscape at our feet—beautiful green fields, enormous trees making spots of black shade in the bright grass, the river, sparkling in the sunshine, winding through the meadows, a group of washerwomen, busy and chattering, beating their clothes on the flat stones where the river narrows a little under the castle walls, and a bright blue sky overhead.

We walked through the Grande Place—picturesque enough. On one side the Church of La Trinité, and in the middle of the Place the bronze equestrian statue of William the Conqueror. It is very spirited. He is in full armor, lance in hand, his horse plunging forward toward imaginary enemies. They say the figure was copied from Queen Mathilde's famous tapestries at Bayeux, but it looked more modern to me. I remember all the men and beasts and ships of those tapestries looked most extraordinary as to shape. Monsieur R. took over the young princesses the other day in his auto. They were very keen to see the cradle of their race. It was curious to see the descendants of the great rough soldier starting in an auto, fresh, pretty English girls, dressed in the trotteuses (little short skirts) that we all wear in the country, carrying their Kodaks and sketching materials.

All this part of the country teems with legends of the great warrior. Years ago, when we were at Deauville, we drove over to Dives to breakfast—one gets a very good breakfast at the little hotel. We wandered about afterward down to the sea (William the Conqueror is said to have sailed from Dives), and into the little church where the names of all the barons who accompanied him to England are written on tablets on the walls. We saw various relics and places associated with him and talked naturally a great deal about the Conqueror. On the way home (we were a large party in a brake) one of our compatriots, a nice young fellow whose early education had evidently not been very comprehensive, turned to me, saying; "Do tell me, what did that fellow conquer?" I could hardly believe my own ears, but unfortunately for him, just at that moment we were walking up a steep hill and everybody in the carriage overheard his remark. It was received with such shouts of laughter that any explanation was difficult, and one may imagine the jokes, and the numerous and fabulous conquests that were instantly put down to the great duke's account. The poor fellow was quite bewildered. However, I don't know if an American is bound to know any history but that of his own country. I am quite sure that many people in the carriage didn't know whom Pocahontas married, nor what part she played in the early days of America. But it was funny all the same.

We have been out again this afternoon in Monsieur R.'s auto—a charming turn. We started out by the Étoile, as Monsieur R. wanted to show it to some gentlemen who were with us. The drive, if anything, was more lovely than the first time, the slanting rays of the sun were so beautiful shining through the rich green foliage, making patterns upon the hard, white road. We raced all over the country, through countless little villages, all exactly alike, sometimes flying past a stately old brick château just seen at the end of a long, beech avenue, sometimes past an old church standing high, its gray stone steeple showing well against the bright, cloudless sky, and a little graveyard stretching along the hillside, the roads bordered on each side with high green banks and hedges, the orchards full of apple-trees, and the whole active population of the village in the fields. It is a beautiful month to be in Normandy, for one must have sun in these parts. As soon as it rains everything is gray and cold and melancholy, the forest looks like a great high black wall, the meadows are shrouded in mist, and the damp strikes through one. Now it is smiling, sunny, peaceful.

We have frightened various horses to-day; a quiet old gray steed, driven by two old ladies in black bonnets. They were too old to get out, and were driving their horse timidly and nervously into the ditch in their anxiety to give us all the road. However, we slowed up and the horse didn't look as if he could run away. Two big carthorses, too, at the end of a long line, dragging a heavy wagon, turned short round and almost ran into us; also a very small donkey, driven by a little brown girl, showed symptoms of flight. I don't know the names of half the villages we passed through. Near Bagnoles we came to La Ferté-Macé, which looks quite imposing as one comes down upon it from the top of a long hill. The church makes a great effect—looks almost like a cathedral. Bagnoles looked very animated as we came back. People were loitering about shopping—quite a number of carriages and autos before the door of the Grand Hotel, and people sitting out under the trees in the gardens of the different villas. It was decidedly cool at the end of our outing; I was glad to have my coat.

This morning after breakfast, in the big hall, where every one congregates for coffee, we had a little political talk—not very satisfactory. Everybody is discontented and everybody protests, but no one seems able to stop the radical current. The rupture with the Vatican has come at last, and I think might have been avoided if they had been a little more patient in Rome. There will be all sorts of complications and bitter feeling, and I don't quite see what benefit the country at large will get from the present state of things. A general feeling of irritation and uncertainty, higher taxes—for they must build school-houses and pay lay-teachers and country curés. A whole generation of children cannot be allowed to grow up without religious instruction of any kind. I can understand how the association of certain religious orders (men) could be mischievous—harmful even—but I am quite sure that no one in his heart believes any harm of the women—soeurs de charité and teachers—who occupy themselves with the old people, the sick, and the children. In our little town they have sent away an old sister who had taught and generally looked after three generations of children. When she was expelled she had been fifty years in the town and was teaching the grandchildren of her first scholars. Everybody knew her, everybody loved her; when any one was ill or in trouble she was always the first person sent for. Now there is at the school an intelligent, well-educated young laïque with all the necessary brevets. I dare say she will teach the children very well, but her task ends with the close of her class. She doesn't go to church, doesn't know the people, doesn't interest herself in all their little affairs, and will never have the position and the influence the old religieuse had.

I am sorry to go away from this quiet little green corner of Normandy, but we have taken the requisite number of baths. Every one rushes off as soon as the last bath (twenty-first generally) is taken. Countess F. took her twenty-first at six o'clock this morning, and left at ten.

IX

A NORMAN TOWN

VALOGNES, August.

I seem to have got into another world, almost another century, in this old town. I had always promised the Florians I would come and stay with them, and was curious to see their installation in one of the fine old hotels of the place. The journey was rather long—not particularly interesting. We passed near Caen, getting a very good view of the two great abbayes[13] with their towers and spires quite sharply outlined against the clear blue sky. The train was full. At almost every station family parties got in—crowds of children all armed with spades, pails, butterfly-nets, and rackets, all the paraphernalia of happy, healthy childhood. For miles after Caen there were long stretches of green pasture-lands—hundreds of cows and horses, some of them the big Norman dray-horses resting a little before beginning again their hard work, and quantities of long-legged colts trotting close up alongside of their mothers, none of them apparently minding the train. We finally arrived at the quiet little station of Valognes. Countess de Florian was waiting for me, with their big omnibus, and we had a short drive all through the town to their hotel, which is quite at one end, a real country road running in front of their house. It is an old hotel standing back from the road and shut in with high iron gates. There is a large court-yard with a grass-plot in the middle, enormous flower-beds on each side, and a fine sweep of carriage road to the perron. A great double stone staircase runs straight up to the top of the house, and glass doors opposite the entrance lead into the garden. I had an impression of great space and height and floods of light. I went straight into the garden, where they gave me tea, which was most refreshing after the long hot day. They have no house party. The dowager countess, Florian's mother, is here, and there was a cousin, a naval officer, who went off to Cherbourg directly after dinner. The ground-floor is charming; on one side of the hall there are three or four salons, and a billiard-room running directly across the house from the garden to the court-yard; on the other, a good dining-room and two or three guests' rooms; the family all live upstairs.

[13] Abbaye aux Hommes, Abbaye aux Dames.

Entrance to hotel of the Comte de Florian.

It is a delightful house. My room is on the ground-floor, opening from the corridor, which is large and bright, paved with flag-stones. My windows look out on the entrance court, so that I see all that goes on. As soon as my maid has opened the windows and brought in my petit déjeuner, I hear a tap at the door and the countess's maid appears to ask, with madame's compliments, if I have all I want, if I have had a good night, and to bring me the morning paper. The first person to move is the dowager countess, who goes to early mass every morning. She is a type of the old-fashioned French Faubourg St. Germain lady; a straight, slender figure, always dressed in black, devoted to her children and to all her own family, with the courteous, high-bred manner one always finds in French women of the old school. She doesn't take much interest in the outside world, nor in anything that goes on in other countries, but is too polite to show that when she talks to me, for instance, who have knocked about so much. She doesn't understand the modern life, so sans gêne and agitated, and it is funny to hear her say when talking of people she doesn't quite approve of, "Ils ne sont pas de notre monde."

Then comes the young countess, very energetic and smiling, with her short skirt and a bag on her arm, going to market. She sees me at the window and stops to know if I am going out. Will I join her at the market? All the ladies of Valognes do their own marketing and some of the well-known fishwomen and farmers' wives who come in from the country with poultry would be quite hurt if Madame la Comtesse didn't come herself to give her orders and have a little talk. This morning I have been to market with Countess Florian. The women looked so nice and clean in their short, black, heavily plaited skirts, high white caps, and handkerchiefs pinned over their bodices. The little stalls went all down the narrow main street and spread out on the big square before the church. The church is large, with a square tower and fine dome—nothing very interesting as to architecture. Some of the stalls were very tempting and the smiling, red-cheeked old women, sitting up behind their wares, were so civil and anxious to sell us something. The fish-market was most inviting—quantities of flat white turbots, shining silver mackerel, and fresh crevettes piled high on a marble slab with water running over them. Four or five short-skirted, bare-legged fisher girls were standing at the door with baskets of fish on their heads. Florian joined us there and seemed on the best of terms with these young women. He made all kinds of jokes with them, to which they responded with giggles and a funny little half-courtesy, half-nod. Both Florians spoke so nicely to all the market people as we passed from stall to stall. The poultry looked very good—such fat ducks and chickens. It was funny to see the bourgeoises of Valognes all armed with a large basket doing their marketing; they looked at the chickens, poked them, lifted them so as to be sure of their weight, and evidently knew to a centime what they had to pay. I fancy the Norman ménagère is a pretty sharp customer and knows exactly what she must pay for everything. The vegetable stalls were very well arranged—the most enormous cabbages I ever saw. I think the old ladies who presided there were doing a flourishing business. I did not find much to buy—some gray knitted stockings that I thought would be good for my Mareuil[14] boys and some blue linen blouses with white embroidery, that all the carters wear, and which the Paris dressmakers

[14] Mareuil is the name of the village near our place in France.

transform into very pretty summer costumes. I bought for myself a paper bag full of cherries for a few sous, then left the Florians, and wandered about the streets a little alone. They are generally narrow, badly paved, with grass growing in the very quiet ones. There are many large hotels standing well back, entre cour et jardin, the big doors and gate-ways generally heavy and much ornamented—a great deal of carving on the façades and cornices, queer heads and beasts. Valognes has not always been the quiet, dull, little provincial town it is to-day. It has had its brilliant moment, when all the hotels were occupied by grands seigneurs, handsome equipages rolled through the streets, and its society prided itself on its exclusiveness and grand manner. It used to be said that to rouler carrosse at Valognes was a titre de noblesse, and the inhabitants considered their town a "petit Paris." In one of the plays of the time, a marquis, very fashionable and a well-known courtier, was made to say: "Il faut trois mois de Valognes pour achever un homme de cour." One can quite imagine "la grande vie d'autrefois" in the hotel of the Florians. Their garden is enchanting—quantities of flowers, roses particularly. They have made two great borders of tall pink rose-bushes, with dwarf palms from Bordighera planted between, just giving the note of stiffness which one would expect to find in an old-fashioned garden. On one side is a large terrace with marble steps and balustrade, and beyond that, half hidden by a row of fruit-trees, a very good tennis court. We just see the church-tower at one end of the garden; and it is so quiet one would never dream there was a town near. The country in every direction is beautiful—real English lanes, the roads low, high banks on each side, with hawthorn bushes on top—one drives between thick green walls. We have made some lovely excursions. They have a big omnibus with a banquette on top which seats four people, also a place by the coachman, and two great Norman posters, who go along at a good steady trot, taking a little gallop occasionally up and down the hills.

Countess de Nadaillac, Countess Florian's sister-in-law, arrived to-day with her daughter for a short visit. We had a pleasant evening with music, billiards, and dominoes (a favorite game in this country). The dowager countess always plays two games, and precisely at half-past nine her old man-servant appears and escorts her to her rooms. We all break up early; the ten o'clock bell is usually the signal. It rings every night, just as it has done for hundreds of years. The town lights are put out and the inhabitants understand that the authorities are not responsible for anything that may happen in the streets of Valognes after such a dangerous hour of the night.

... There are some fine places in the neighborhood. We went to-day to Chiffevast, a large château which had belonged to the Darus, but has been bought recently by a rich couple, Valognes people, who have made a large fortune in cheese and butter. It seems their great market is London.

They send over quantities via Cherbourg, which is only twenty minutes off by rail. It is a splendid place—with a fine approach by a great avenue with beautiful old trees. The château is a large, square house—looks imposing as one drives up. We didn't see the master of the house—he was away—but madame received us in all her best clothes. She was much better dressed than we were, evidently by one of the good Paris houses. Countess Florian had written to ask if we might come, so she was under arms. She was a little nervous at first, talked a great deal, very fast, but when she got accustomed to us it went more easily, and she showed us the house with much pride. There was some good furniture and one beautiful coverlet of old lace and embroidery, which she had found somewhere upstairs in an old chest of drawers. They have no children—such a pity, as they are improving and beautifying the place all the time. The drive home was delightful, facing the sunset. I was amused with the Florians' old coachman. He is a curiosity—knows everybody in the country. He was much interested in our visit and asked if we had seen "la patronne"—said he knew her well, had often seen her on a market day at Valognes, sitting in her little cart in the midst of her cheeses and butter; said she was a brave femme. How strange it must seem to people like that, just out of their hard-working peasant life—and it *is* hard work in France—to find themselves owners of a splendid château and estate, receiving the great people of the country. I dare say in ten or twelve years they will be like any one else, and if there were sons or daughters the young men would get into parliament or the diplomatic career, the daughters would marry some impoverished scion of a noble family, and cheeses and butter would be forgotten.

We had one delightful day at Cherbourg. The Préfet Maritime invited us to breakfast with him at his hotel. We went by rail to Cherbourg, about half an hour, and found the admiral's carriage waiting for us. The prefecture is a nice, old-fashioned house, in the centre of the town, with a big garden. We took off our coats in a large, handsome room upstairs. The walls were covered with red damask and there were pictures of Queen Victoria and Louis Napoleon. It seems the Queen slept in that room one night when she came over to France to make her visit to Louis Philippe at the Château d'Eu. We found quite a party assembled—all the men in uniform and the women generally in white. We breakfasted in a large dining-room with glass doors opening into the garden, which was charming, a blaze of bright summer flowers. We adjourned there for coffee after breakfast. The trees were big, made a good shade, and the little groups, seated about in the various bosquets, looked pretty and gay. When coffee and liqueurs were finished we drove down to the quay, where the admiral's launch was waiting, and had a delightful afternoon steaming about the harbour. It is enormous, long jetties and breakwaters stretching far out, almost closing it in. There was every description of craft—big Atlantic liners, yachts, fishing boats, ironclads, torpedoes, and once we very nearly ran over a curious dark object floating on the surface of the water, which they told us was a submarine. It did not look comfortable as a means of transportation, but the young officers told us it was delightful.

We got back to Valognes to a late dinner, having invited a large party to come over for tennis and dinner the next day. The Florians are a godsend to Cherbourg. They are most hospitable, and with automobiles the distance is nothing, and one is quite independent of trains. Yesterday four of our party went off to Cherbourg to make a cruise in a torpedo-boat. The ladies were warned that they must put on clothes which would not mind sea-water, but I should think bathing dresses would be the only suitable garments for such an expedition. They were remarkable objects when they came home, Mademoiselle de Nadaillac's hat a curiosity, also her white blouse, where the red of her hat-ribbons and cravat had run. However, they had enjoyed themselves immensely—at least the girl. Countess de Nadaillac was not quite so enthusiastic. They got into dry clothes and played tennis vigorously all the afternoon.

Market women. Valognes.

We had a pleasant family evening. Mademoiselle de Nadaillac has a pretty voice and sang well. Florian and I played some duets. I joined in the dowager's game of dominoes, which I don't seem to have mastered, as I lose regularly, and after she left us, escorted by her faithful old butler (a light shawl over his arm to put on her shoulders when she passed through the corridors), we had rather an interesting conversation about ways and manners in different countries, particularly the way young people are brought up. I said we were a large family and that mother would never let us read in the drawing-room after dinner. If we were all absorbed in our books, conversation was impossible. We were all musical, so the piano and singing helped us through. Madame de Florian, whose father, Marquis de Nadaillac, is quite of the old school, said they were not even allowed to work or look at pictures in the *salon* after dinner! Her father considered it disrespectful if any of his children did anything but listen when he talked. They might join in the conversation if they had anything intelligent to say. She told us, too, of some of the quite old-fashioned châteaux that she stayed in as a girl, and even a young married woman. There was one fire and one lamp in the drawing-room. Any one who wanted to be warm, or to work, was obliged to come into that room. No fires nor lamps allowed anywhere else in the house; a cup of tea in the afternoon an unheard-of luxury. If you were ill, a doctor was sent for and he ordered a tisane; if you were merely tired or cold, you waited until dinner-time.

We have also made a charming expedition to Quinéville, a small seaside place about an hour and a half's drive, always through the same green country, our Norman posters galloping up all the hills. We passed through various little villages, each one with a pretty little gray, square-towered church. There was plenty of passing, as it was market day. We met a good many peasant women carrying milk in those curious old brass bowls one sees everywhere here. Some of them are very handsome, polished until they shine like mirrors, with a delicate pattern lightly traced running around the bowl. They balance them perfectly on their heads and walk along at a good swinging pace. They all look prosperous, their skirts (generally black), shoes, and stockings in good condition, and their white caps and handkerchiefs as clean as possible. Quinéville is a very quiet little place, no hotel, and rows of ugly little houses well back from the sea, but there is a beautiful stretch of firm white sand. To-day it was dead low tide. The sea looked miles away, a long line of dark sea-weed marking the water's edge. There were plenty of people about; women and girls with stout bare legs, and a primitive sort of tool, half pitchfork, half shovel, were piling the sea-weed into the carts which were waiting on the shore. Children were paddling about in the numerous little pools and making themselves wreaths and necklaces out of the berries of the sea-weed—some of them quite bright-coloured, pink and yellow. We wandered about on the beach, sitting sometimes on the side of a boat, and walking through the little pools and streams. It was a lonely bit of water. We didn't see a sail. The sea looked like a great blue plain meeting the sky—nothing to break the monotony. We got some very bad coffee at the restaurant—didn't attempt tea. They would certainly have *said* they had it, and would have made it probably out of hay from the barn. The drive home was delicious, almost too cool, as we went at a good pace, the horses knowing as well as we did that the end of their day was coming.... We have been again to market this morning. It was much more amusing than the first time, as it was horse day, and men and beasts were congregated in the middle of the Cathedral Square. There was a fair show—splendid big cart-horses and good cobs and ponies—here and there a nice saddle-horse. There were a good many women driving themselves, and almost all had good, stout little horses. They know just as much about it as the men and were much interested in the sales. They told me the landlady of the hotel was the best judge of a horse and a *man* in Normandy. She was standing at the entrance of her court-yard as we passed the hotel on our way home, a comely, buxom figure, dressed like all the rest in a short black skirt and sabots. She was exchanging smiling greetings and jokes with every one who passed and keeping order with the crowds of farmers, drivers, and horse-dealers who were jostling through the big open doors and clamoring for food for themselves and their animals. She was the type of the hard-working, capable Frenchwoman of whom there are thousands in France.

Some years ago I was on the committee for a great sale we had in our arrondissement in Paris for the benefit of "L'Assistance par le Travail," an excellent work which we are all much interested in. I was in charge of the buffet, and thought it better to apply at once to one of the great caterers, Potel and Chabot, and see what they could do for us. We made an appointment, and Mme. de B. and I drove down to the place. The manager was out, but they told us that Madame was waiting for us in the back shop. We found rather a pretty woman, very well dressed in velvet, with diamond ear-rings, and I was put out at first—thought that didn't look like business. However, we talked a few minutes; she said her husband was obliged to go to the country, but would certainly come and see me the next day. Then she stepped up to her desk, where there was a big book open, said she understood we wished to give an order for a buffet for a charity sale, and was at once absorbed in sandwiches, tea and coffee, orangeade, and all the requirements for such an occasion. She was perfectly practical and gave us some very useful hints—said she supposed we wanted some of their maîtres d'hôtel. We thought not—our own would do. That, she said, would be a great mistake. They weren't accustomed to that sort of thing and wouldn't know how to do it. One thing, for instance—they would certainly fill all the glasses of orangeade and punch much too full and would waste a great deal. Their men never filled a glass entirely, and consequently gained two on every dozen. She told us how much we wanted, made out the estimate at once, and ended by asking if we would allow them to present the tea as their contribution to the charity. It didn't take more than twenty minutes—the whole thing. She then shut up her book, went to the door with us, thanked us for giving them the order, and hoped we would be satisfied. That business capability and thriftiness runs through almost all Frenchwomen of a certain class, and when I hear, as of course I often do, the frivolous, butterfly, pleasure-loving Frenchwoman spoken of, that energetic, hard-working bourgeoise comes into my mind. We all who live in France know the type well.

The whole nation is frugal. During the Franco-German War, my husband, who had spent all the dreary months of the invasion at his château in the country, was elected a member of the Assemblée Nationale, which met at Bordeaux. They were entirely cut off from Paris, surrounded by Prussian troops on all sides, and he couldn't get any money. Whatever he had had at the beginning of the war had been spent—sending off recruits for one of the great army corps near his place. It was impossible to communicate with his banker or any friends in Paris, and yet he couldn't start without funds. He applied to the notary of La Ferté-Milon, the little town nearest the château. He asked how much he wanted. W. said about 10,000 francs. The notary said, "Give me two days and I will get it for you." He appeared three days afterward, bringing the 10,000 francs—a great deal of it in large silver five-franc pieces, very difficult to carry. He had collected the whole sum from small farmers and peasants in the neighbourhood—the five-franc pieces coming always from the peasants, sometimes fifty sewed up in a mattress or in the woman's thick, wadded Sunday skirt. He said he could get as much more if W. wanted it. It seems impossible for the peasant to part with his money or invest it. He must keep it well hidden, but in his possession.

... We had a pretty drive this afternoon to one of Florian's farms, down a little green lane, some distance from the high-road and so hidden by the big trees that we saw nothing until we got close to the gate. It was late—all the cows coming home, the great Norman horses drinking at the trough, two girls with bare legs and high caps calling all the fowl to supper, and the farmer's wife, with a baby in her arms and another child, almost a baby, pulling at her skirts, seated on a stone bench underneath a big apple-tree, its branches heavy with fruit. She was superintending the work of the farm-yard and seeing that the two girls didn't waste a minute of their time, nor a grain of the seed with which they were feeding the chickens. A little clear, sparkling stream was meandering through the meadows, tall poplars on each side, and quite at the end of the stretch of green fields there was the low blue line of the sea. The farm-house is a large, old-fashioned building with one or two good rooms. It had evidently been a small manor house. One of the rooms is charming, with handsome panels of dark carved wood. It seemed a pity to leave them there, and almost a pity that the Florians could not have made their home in such a lovely green spot, but they would have been obliged to add to the house enormously, and it would have complicated their lives, being so far away from everything.

... We have had a last walk and flânerie this morning. We went to the Hospice, formerly a Benedictine convent, where there is a fine gate-way and court-yard with most extraordinary carving over the doors and gate—monstrous heads and beasts and emblems alongside of cherubs and beautiful saints and angels. One wonders what ideas those old artists had; it seems now such distorted imagination. We walked through some of the oldest streets and past what had been fine hotels, but they are quite uninhabited now. Sometimes a bric-à-brac shop on the ground-floor, and some sort of society on the upper story, but they are all neglected and half tumbling down. There is still splendid carving on some of the old gate-ways and cornices, but bits of stone and plaster are falling off, grass is growing between the paving stones of the court-yards, and there is an air of poverty and neglect which is a curious contrast to the prosperous look of the country all around—all the little farms and villages look so thriving. The people are smiling and well fed;

their animals, too—horses, cows, donkeys—all in good condition.

I have played my last game of dominoes in this fine old hotel and had my last cup of tea in the stiff, stately garden, with the delicious salt sea-breeze always coming at four o'clock, and the cathedral chimes sounding high and clear over our heads. I leave to-morrow night for London, via Cherbourg and Southampton.

Old gate-way. Valogues.

X

NORMAN CHATEAUX

We never remained all summer at our place. August was a disagreeable month there—the woods were full of horse-flies which made riding impossible. No nets could keep them off the horses who were almost maddened by the sting. They were so persistent that we had to take them off with a sharp stick. They stuck like leeches. We generally went to the sea—almost always to the Norman Coast—establishing ourselves in a villa—sometimes at Deauville, sometimes at Villers, and making excursions all over the country.

Some of the old Norman châteaux are charming, particularly those which have remained just as they were before the Revolution, but, of course, there are not many of these. When the young ones succeed, there is always a tendency to modify and change, and it is not easy to mix the elaborate luxurious furniture of our times with the stiff old-fashioned chairs and sofas one finds in the old French houses. Merely to look at them one understands why our grandfathers and grandmothers always sat upright.

One of the most interesting of the Norman châteaux is "Abondant," in the department of the Eure-et-Loir, belonging until very recently to the Vallambrosa family. It belonged originally to la Duchesse de Tourzel, gouvernante des Enfants de France (children of Louis XVI and Marie Antoinette). After the imprisonment of the Royal Family, Madame de Tourzel retired to her château d'Abondant and remained there all through the Revolution. The village people and peasants adored her and she lived there peacefully through all those terrible days. Neither château nor park was damaged in any way, although she was known to be a devoted friend and adherent of the unfortunate Royal Family. A band of half-drunken "patriots" tried to force their way into the park one day, with the intention of cutting down the trees and pillaging the château, but all the villagers instantly assembled, armed with pitchforks, rusty old guns and stones, and dispersed the rabble.

Abondant is a Louis XV château—very large—seventeen rooms en façade—but simple in its architecture. The Duchess occupied a large corner room on the ground-floor, with four windows. The ceiling (which was very high) and walls covered with toiles de Jouy. An enormous bed à baldaquin was trimmed with the same toile and each post had a great bunch of white feathers on top.

In 1886, when one of my friends was staying at Abondant, the hangings were the same which had been there all through the Revolution. She told me she had never been so miserable as the first time she stayed at the château during the lifetime of the late Duchesse de Vallambrosa. They gave her the Duchesse de Tourzel's room, thinking it would interest her as a chambre historique. She was already nervous at sleeping alone on the ground-floor, far from all the other inmates of the château. The room was enormous—walls nearly five metres high—the bed looked like an island in the midst of space; there was very little furniture, and the white feathers on the bed-posts nodded and waved in the dim light. She scarcely closed her eyes, could not reason with herself, and asked the next morning to have something less magnificent and more modern.

In all the bedrooms the dressing-tables were covered with dentelle de Binche[15] of the epoch, and all the mirrors and various little boxes for powder, rouge, patches, and the hundred accessories for a fine lady's toilette in those days, were in Vernis Martin absolutely intact. The drawing-rooms still had their old silk hangings—a white ground covered with wreaths of flowers and birds with wonderful bright plumage—hand-painted—framed in wood of two shades of light green.

The big drawing-room was entirely panelled in wood of the same light green, most beautifully and delicately carved. These old boiseries were all removed when the château was sold. After the death of the Duchesse de Tourzel the château went to her niece, the Duchesse des Cars—who left it to her niece, the Duchesse de Vallambrosa, a very rare instance, in France, of a property descending directly through several generations in the female line.

It was sold by the Vallambrosas. The old wood panels are in the Paris house of a member of that family. The park was very large and beautifully laid out, with the fine trees one sees all over Normandy.

Twenty years ago a salle de spectacle "en verdure" still existed in the park—the seats were all in grass; the coulisses (side scenes) made in the trees of the park—their boughs cut and trained into shape, to represent green walls, a marble group of allegorical figures at the back. It was most carefully preserved—the seats of the amphitheatre looked like green velvet and the trees were always cut in the same curious shapes. It seemed quite a fitting part of the fine old place, with its memories of past fêtes and splendours, before the whirlwind of liberty and equality swept over the country.

Many of the châteaux are changing hands. The majorat (entail) doesn't exist in France, and as the fortunes must always be divided among the children, it becomes more and more difficult to keep up the large places. Life gets dearer every day—fortunes don't increase—very few young Frenchmen of the upper classes do anything. The only way of keeping up the big places is by making a rich marriage—the daughter of a rich banker or industrial, or an American.

Our cousins, Comte and Comtesse d'Y——, have a pretty little old place not very far from Villers-sur-Mer, where we went sometimes for sea-bathing. The house is an ordinary square white stone building, a fine terrace with a flight of steps leading down to the garden on one side. The park is delightful—many splendid old trees. Until a few years ago there were still some that dated since Louis

[15] Binche, name of a village in Belgium where the lace is made.

XIV. The last one of that age—a fine oak, with wide spreading branches—died about two years ago, but they cannot make up their minds to cut it down. I advised them to leave the trunk standing—(I think, by degrees, the branches will fall as they are quite dead)—cover it with ivy or a vine of some kind, and put a notice on it of the age of the tree.

The house stands high, and they have splendid views—on one side, from the terrace, a great expanse of green valley looking toward Falaise—on the other, the sea—a beautiful, blue summer sea, when we were there the other day.

We went over from Villers to breakfast. It was late in the season, the end of September—one of those bright days one sometimes has in September, when summer still lingers and the sun gives beautiful mellow tints to everything without being strong enough to make one feel the heat. The road was lovely all the way, particularly after we turned off the high road at the top of the Houlgate Hill. We went through countless little Norman lanes, quite narrow, sometimes—between high green banks with a hedge on top, and the trees meeting over our heads—so narrow that I wondered what would happen if we met another auto. We left the sea behind us, and plunged into the lovely green valley that runs along back of the coast line. We came suddenly on the gates of the château, rather a sharp turn. There was a broad avenue with fine trees leading up to the house—on one side, meadows fenced off with white wooden palings where horses and cows were grazing—a pretty lawn before the house with beds of begonias, and all along the front, high raised borders of red geranium which looked very well against the grey stone.

We found a family party, Comte and Comtesse d'Y— —, their daughter and a governess. We went upstairs (a nice wooden staircase with broad shallow steps) to an end room, with a beautiful view over the park, where we got out of all the wraps, veils, and glasses that one must have in an open auto if one wishes to look respectable when one arrives, and went down at once to the hall where the family was waiting.

The dining-room was large and light, high, wide windows and beautiful trees wherever one looked. The decoration of the room was rather curious. The d'Y— —s descend—like many Norman families—from William the Conqueror, and there are English coats-of-arms on some of the shields on the walls. A band which looks like fresco, but is really painted on linen—very cleverly arranged with some composition which makes it look like the wall—runs straight around the room with all sorts of curious figures: soldiers, horses, and boats, copied exactly from the famous Bayeux tapestries, the most striking episodes—the departure of the Conqueror from Dives—the embarkation of his army (the cavalry—most extraordinary long queerly shaped horses with faces like people)—the death of Harold—the fighting Bishop Odo—brother of the Conqueror, who couldn't carry a lance, but had a good stout stick which apparently did good service as various Saxons were flying horizontally through the air as he and his steed advanced; one wonders at the imagination which could have produced such extraordinary figures, as certainly no men or beasts, at any period of time, could have looked like those. The ships were less striking—had rather more the semblance of boats.

However, the effect, with all the bright colouring, is very good and quite in harmony with this part of the country, where everything teems with legends and traditions of the great Duke. They see Falaise, where he was born, from their terrace, sometimes. We didn't, for though the day was beautiful, there was a slight haze which made the far-off landscapes only a blue line.

After breakfast we went for a walk in the park. They have arranged it very well, with rustic bridges and seats wherever the view was particularly fine. We saw a nice, old, red brick house, near the farm, which was the manoir where the Dowager Countess lives now. She made over the château to her son, in her life time, on condition that he would keep it up and arrange it, which he has done very well. We made the tour of the park—passing a pretty lodge with roses and creepers all over it and "Mairie" put upon a sign; d'Y— —is mayor of his little village and finds it convenient to have the Mairie at his own gate. We rested a little in the drawing-room before going back, and he showed us various portraits and miniatures of his family which were most interesting. Some of the miniatures are exactly like one we have of father, of that period with the high stock and tight-buttoned coat. The light was lovely—so soft and warm—in the drawing-room, and as there were no lace curtains or vitrages, and the silk curtains were drawn back from the high plate glass windows, we seemed to be sitting in the park under the trees. They gave us tea and the good little cakes, "St. Pierre," a sort of "sablé," for which all the coast is famous.

The drive home was enchanting, with a lovely view from the top of the hill; a beautiful blue sea at our feet and the turrets and pointed roofs of the Villers houses taking every possible colour from the sunset clouds.

We went back once more to a thé dansant given for her seventeen-year-old daughter. It was a lovely afternoon and the place looked charming—the gates open—carriages and autos arriving in every direction—people came from a great distance as with the autos no one hesitates to undertake a drive of a hundred kilomètres. The young people danced in the drawing-room—Madame d'Y— — had taken out all the furniture, and the parents and older people sat about on the terrace where there were plenty of seats and little tea-tables. The dining-room—with an abundant buffet—was always full; one arrives with a fine appetite after whirling for two or three hours through the keen salt air. The girls all looked charming—the white dresses, bright sashes, and big picture hats are so becoming. They were dancing hard when we left, about half past six, and it was a pretty sight as we looked back from the gates—long lines of sunlight wavering over the grass, figures in white flitting through the trees, distant strains of music, and what was less agreeable, the strident sound of a sirène on some of the autos. They are detestable things.

We were very comfortable at Villers in a nice, clean house looking on the sea, with broad balconies at every story, where we put sofas and tables and green blinds, using them as extra salons. We were never in the house except to eat and sleep. Nothing is more characteristic of the French (particularly in the bourgeoise) than the thorough way in which they *do* their month at the sea-shore. They generally come for the month of August. Holidays have begun and business, of all kinds, is slack. Our plage was really a curiosity. There is a splendid stretch of sand beach—at low tide one can walk, by the shore, to Trouville or Houlgate on perfectly firm, dry sand. There are hundreds of cabins and tents, striped red and white, and umbrellas on the beach, and all day long whole families sit there. They all bathe, and a curious fashion at Villers is that you put on your bathing dress in your own house—over that a peignoir, generally of red and white striped cotton, and walk quite calmly through the streets to the établissement. Some of the ladies and gentlemen of mature years are not to their advantage. When they can, if they have houses with a terrace or garden, they take their meals outside, and as soon as they have breakfasted, start again for the beach. When it is low tide they go shrimp-fishing or walk about in the shallow water looking for shells and sea-weed. When it is high tide, all sit at the door of their tents sewing, reading, or talking—I mean, of course, the petite bourgeoisie.

At other places on the coast, Deauville or Houlgate, the life is like Newport or Dinard, or any other fashionable sea-side place, with automobiles, dinners, dressing, etc. They get all the sea air and out-of-door life that they can crowd into one month. One lady said to me one day, "I can't bathe, but I take a 'bain d'air' every day—I sit on the rocks as far out in the water as I can—take off my hat and my shoes and stockings."

There is a great clearing out always by the first of September and then the place was enchanting—bright, beautiful September days, one could still bathe, the sun was so strong; and the afternoons, with just a little chill in the air, were delightful for walking and driving. There was a pretty Norman farm—just over the plage—at the top of the falaise where we went sometimes for tea. They gave us very good tea, milk, and cider, and excellent bread and butter and cheese. We sat out of doors in an apple orchard at little tables—all the beasts of the establishment in the same field. The chickens and sheep surrounded us, were evidently accustomed to being fed, but the horses, cows, and calves kept quite to the other end. We saw the girls milking the cows which, of course, interested the children immensely.

We made some charming excursions in the auto—went one Saturday to Caen—such a pretty road through little smiling villages—every house with a garden, or if too close together to allow that, there were pots of geraniums, the falling kind, in the windows, which made a red curtain dropping down over the walls. We stopped at Lisieux—a quaint old Norman town, with a fine cathedral and curious houses with gables and towers—one street most picturesque, very narrow, with wooden houses, their projecting roofs coming so far over the street one could hardly see the sky in some places. There were all kinds of balconies and cornices most elaborately carved—the wood so dark one could scarcely distinguish the original figures and devices, but some of them were extraordinary, dragons, and enormous winged animals. We did not linger very long as we were in our new auto—a Martini hill-climber—built in Switzerland and, of course (like all automobilists), were anxious to make as fast a run as possible between Villers and Caen.

The approach to Caen is not particularly interesting—the country is flat, the road running through poplar-bordered fields—one does not see it at all until one gets quite near, and then suddenly beautiful towers and steeples seem to rise out of the green meadows. It was Saturday—market day—and the town was crowded—every description of vehicle in the main street and before the hotel, two enormous red 60-horse-power Mercedes—farmers' gigs and donkey carts with cheeses and butter—a couple generally inside—the man with his blue smock and broad-brimmed hat, the woman with a high, clean, stiff-starched muslin cap, a knit shawl over her shoulders. They were not in the least discomposed by the bustle and the automobiles, never thought of getting out of the way—jogged comfortably on keeping to their side of the road.

We left the auto at the hotel and found many others in the court-yard, and various friends. The d'Y— —s had come over from Grangues (their place). He is Conseiller Général of Calvados, and market day, in a provincial town, is an excellent occasion for seeing one's electors. There were also some friends from Trouville-Deauville, most of them in autos—some in light carriages. We tried to make a rendezvous for tea at the famous pâtissier's (who sends his cakes and bonbons over half the department), but that was not very practical, as they had all finished what they had to do and we had not even begun our sightseeing. However, d'Y— — told us he would leave our names at the tea-room, a sort of club they have established over the pâtissier's, where we would be quieter and better served than in the shop which would certainly be crowded on Saturday afternoon. We walked about till we were dead tired.

St. Pierre is a fine old Norman church with beautiful tower and steeple. It stands fairly well in the Place St. Pierre, but the houses are much too near. It should have more space around it. There was a market going on, on the other side of the square—fruit, big apples and pears, flowers and fish being heaped up together. The apples looked tempting, such bright red ones.

We went to the two abbayes—both of them quite beautiful—St. Étienne—Abbaye aux Hommes was built by William the Conqueror, who was originally buried there. It is very grand—quite simple, but splendid proportions—a fitting resting-place for the great soldier, who, however, was not allowed to sleep his last sleep, undisturbed, in the city he loved so well. His tomb was desecrated several times and his remains lost in the work of destruction.

We went on to the Abbaye aux Dames which is very different; smaller—not nearly so simple. The façade is very fine with two square towers most elaborately carved, the steeples have long since disappeared; and there are richly ornamented galleries and balustrades in the interior of the church, not at all the high solemn vaulted aisles of the Abbaye aux Hommes. It was founded by Queen Mathilde, wife of William the Conqueror, and she is buried there—a perfectly simple tomb with an inscription in Latin. There was at one time a very handsome monument, but it was destroyed, like so many others, during the Revolution, and the remains placed, some years after, in the stone coffin where they now rest. We hadn't time to see the many interesting things in the churches and in the town, as it was getting late and we wanted some tea before we started back. We found our way to the pâtissier's quite easily, but certainly couldn't have had any tea if d'Y— — had not told us to use his name and ask for the club-room. The little shop was crowded—people standing and making frantic dashes into the kitchen for chocolate and muffins. The club-room upstairs was quite nice—painted white, a good glass so that we could arrange our hair a little, one or two tables—and we were attended to at once. They brought us the spécialité of the place—light, hot brioches with grated ham inside—very good and very indigestible.

We went home by a different road, but it looked just like the other—fewer little hamlets, perhaps, and great pasture fields, filled with fine specimens of Norman dray horses and mares with long-legged colts running alongside of them. It was late when we got home. The lighthouses of Honfleur and Havre made a long golden streak stretching far out to sea, and the great turning flashlight of St. Adresse was quite dazzling.

We went back over the same ground two or three days later on our way to Bayeux. The town is not particularly interesting, but the cathedral is beautiful and in wonderful preservation—the columns are very grand—every capital exquisitely carved and no two alike. Our guide, a very talkative person—unlike the generality of Norman peasants, who are usually taciturn—was very anxious to show us each column in detail and explain all the really beautiful carving, but we were rather hurried as some of the party were going to lunch at Barbieville—Comte Foy's château.

On the same place as the cathedral is the Hôtel de Ville, with the wonderful tapestries worked by the Queen Mathilde, wife of William the Conqueror. They are really most extraordinary and so well preserved. The colours look as if they had been painted yesterday. I hadn't seen them for years and had forgotten the curious shapes and vivid colouring. We went to one of the lace shops. The Bayeux lace is very pretty, made with the "fuseau," very fine—a mixture of Valenciennes and Mechlin. It is very strong, though it looks delicate. The dentellières still do a very good business. The little girls begin to work as soon as they can thread their needle, and follow a simple pattern.

The F.'s enjoyed their day at Barbieville, Comte Foy's château, very much. They said the house was nothing remarkable—a large square building, but the park was original. Comte Foy is a racing man, breeds horses, and has his "haras" on his place. The park is all cut up into paddocks, each one separated from the other by a hedge and all connected by green paths. F. said the effect from the terrace was quite charming; one saw nothing but grass and hedges and young horses and colts running about. Comtesse Foy and her daughters were making lace. The girls went in to Bayeux three or four times a week and took lessons from one of the dentellières.

XI

BOULOGNE-SUR-MER

One year we were at Boulogne for the summer in a funny little house, in a narrow street just behind the port and close to the Casino and beach. There were a great many people—all the hotels full and quantities of automobiles passing all day. The upper part of the town is just like any other seaside place—rows of hotels and villas facing the sea—some of the houses built into the high green cliff which rises steep and almost menacing behind. Already parts of the cliff have crumbled away in some place and the proprietors of the villas find some difficulty in letting them. The front rooms on the sea are charming, but the back ones—directly under the cliff—with no air or sun, are not very tempting. There is a fine digue and raised broad walk all along the sea front, with flowers, seats, and music stand.

It is a perfectly safe beach for children, for though the channel is very near and the big English boats pass close to the shore, there are several sand banks which make the beach quite safe, and from seven in the morning till seven at night there are two boats au large and two men on the beach, with ropes, life-preservers, and horns which they blow whenever they think the bathers are too far out. There is an "Inspecteur de la Plage," a regular French official with a gold band on his cap, who is a most important and amiable gentleman and sees that no one is annoyed in any way. We made friends with him at once, moyennant une pièce de dix francs, and he looked after us, saw that our tents were put up close to the water, no others near, and warned off stray children and dogs who were attracted by our children's toys and cakes.

The plage is a pretty sight on a bright day. There are hundreds of tents—all bright-coloured. When one approaches Boulogne from the sea the beach looks like a parterre of flowers. Near the Casino there are a quantity of old-fashioned ramshackly bathing cabins on wheels, with very small boys cracking their whips and galloping up and down, from the digue to the edge of the water, on staid old horses who know their work perfectly—put themselves at once into the shafts of the carriages—never go beyond a certain limit in the sea.

All the bathers are prudent. It is rare to see any one swimming out or diving from a boat. A policeman presides at the public bathing place and there are three or four baigneurs and baigneuses who take charge of the timid bathers; one wonderful old woman, bare-legged, of course, a handkerchief on her head, a flannel blouse and a very short skirt made of some water-proof material that stood out stiff all around her and shed the water—she was the première baigneuse—seventy years old and had been baigneuse at Boulogne for fifty-one years. She had bathed C. as a child, and was delighted to see her again and wildly interested in her two children.

There were donkeys, of course, and goats. The children knew the goat man well and all ran to him with their mugs as soon as they heard his peculiar whistle. They held their mugs close under the goat so that they got their milk warm and foaming, as it was milked directly into their mugs. The goats were quite tame—one came always straight to our tents and lay down there till his master came. Every one wanted to feed them with cakes and bits of sugar, but he would never let them have anything for fear it should spoil their milk.

Another friend was the cake man, dressed all in white, with his basket of brioches and madeleines on his head—then there were the inevitable Africans with fezes on their heads and bundles of silks—crêpes-de-chine and ostrich feathers, that one sees at every plage. I don't think they did much business.

The public was not all distinguished. We often wondered where the people were who lived in the hôtels (all very expensive) and villas, for, with very rare exceptions, it was the most ordinary petite bourgeoisie that one saw on the beach—a few Americans, a great many fourth-rate English. They were a funny contrast to the people who came for the Concours Hippique, and the Race Week. One saw then a great influx of automobiles—there were balls at the Casino and many pretty, well-dressed women, of both worlds, much en evidence. The châtelains from the neighbouring châteaux appeared and brought their guests.

For that one week Boulogne was quite fashionable. The last Sunday of the races was a terrible day. There was an excursion train from Paris and two excursion steamers from England. We were on the quay when the English boats came in and it was amusing to see the people. Some of them had left London at six in the morning. There were all sorts and kinds, wonderful sportsmen with large checked suits, caps and field glasses slung over their shoulders—a great many pretty girls—generally in white. All had bags and baskets with bathing suits and luncheon, and in an instant they were swarming over the plage—already crowded with the Paris excursionists. They didn't interfere with us much as we never went to the beach on Sunday.

F. was fishing all day with some of his friends in a pilot boat. (They brought back three hundred mackerel), had a beautiful day—the sea quite calm and the fish rising in quantities. C. and I, with the children, went off to the Hardelot woods in the auto. We established ourselves on a hillside, pines all around us, the sea at our feet, a beautiful blue sky overhead, and not a sound to break the stillness except sometimes, in the distance, the sirène of a passing auto. We had our tea-basket, found a nice clear space to make a fire, which we did very prudently, scooping out a great hole in the ground and making a sort of oven. It was very difficult to keep the children from tumbling into the hole as they were rolling about on the soft ground, but we got home without any serious detriment to life or limb.

The life in our quarter on the quais is very different, an extraordinary animation and movement. There are hundreds of vessels of every description in the port. All day and all night boats are coming in and going out: The English steamers with their peculiar, dull, penetrating whistle that one hears at a great distance—steam tugs that take passengers and luggage out to the Atlantic liners, lying just outside the digue—yachts, pilot boats, easily distinguished by a broad white line around their hulls, and a number very conspicuously printed in large black letters on their white sails, "baliseurs," smart-looking little craft that take buoys out to the various points where they must be laid. One came in the other day with two large, red, bell-shaped buoys on her deck which made a great effect from a distance; we were standing on the pier, and couldn't imagine what they were; "avisos" (dispatch-boats), with their long, narrow flamme, which marks them as war vessels, streaming out in the wind. Their sailors looked very picturesque in white jerseys and blue bérets with red pompons. Small steamers that run along the coast from Calais to Dunkirk—others, cargo boats, broad and deep in the water, that take fruit and eggs over to England. The baskets of peaches, plums, and apricots look most appetizing when they are taken on board. The steamers look funny when they come back with empty baskets, quantities of them, piled up on the decks, tied to the masts. Many little pleasure boats—flat, broad rowing boats that take one across the harbour to the Gare Maritime (which is a long way around by the bridge), a most uncomfortable performance at low tide, as you go down long, steep, slippery steps with no railing, and have to scramble into the boat as well as you can.

Of course, there are fishing-boats of every description, from the modest little sloop with one mast and small sail to the big steam trawlers which are increasing every year and gradually replacing the old-fashioned sailing-boat. One always knows when the fishing-boats are arriving by the crowd that assembles on the quay; that peculiar population that seems natural to all ports, young, able-bodied sailors, full of interest about the run and the cargo—old men in blue jerseys who sit on the wall, in the sun, all day, and recount their experiences—various officials with gold bands on their caps, men with hand carts waiting to carry off the fish and fishwives—their baskets strapped on their backs—hoping for a haul of crabs and shrimps or fish from some of the small boats.

All the cargo of the trawlers is sold before they arrive to the marieurs (men who deal exclusively in fish), and who have a contract with the big boats. There is no possibility of having a good fish except at the Halles, where one can sometimes get some from one of the smaller boats, which fish on their own account and have no contract; but even those are generally sold at once to small dealers, who send them off to the neighbouring inland towns. In fact, the proprietor of one of the big hotels told me he had to get his fish from Paris and paid Paris prices.

The fishwives, the young ones particularly, are a fine-looking lot—tall, straight, with feet and legs bare, a little white cap or woollen fichu on their heads—they carry off their heavy baskets as lightly as possible, taking them to the Halles where all the fish must go. They are quite a feature of Boulogne, the young fishwives. One sees them often at low tide—fishing for shrimps, carrying their heavy nets on their shoulders and flat baskets strapped on their backs into which they tip the fish very cleverly. They are quite distinct from the Boulonaises matelottes, who are a step higher in the social scale. *They* always wear a wonderful white cap with a high starched frill which stands out around their faces like an auréole. They, too, wear short full skirts, but have long stockings and very good stout *shoes*—not sabots—which are also disappearing. They turn out very well on Sundays. I saw a lot of them the other day coming out of church—all with their caps scrupulously clean—short, full, black or brown skirts; aprons ironed in a curious way—*across* the apron—making little waves (our maids couldn't think what had happened to their white aprons the first time they came back from the wash—thought there had been some mistake and they had some one's else clothes—they had to explain to the washerwoman that they liked their aprons ironed straight); long gold earrings and gold chains. They are handsome women, dark with straight features, a serious look in their eyes. Certainly people who live by the sea have a different expression—there is something grave, almost sad in their faces, which one doesn't see in dwellers in sunny meadows and woodlands.

We went this morning with the Baron de G., who is at the head of one of the fishing companies here, to see one of their boats come in and unload. It was a steam trawler, with enormous nets, that had been fishing off the English coast near Land's End. There were quite a number of people assembled on the quay—a policeman, a garde du port, an agent of the company, and the usual lot of people who are always about when a fishing-boat comes in. Her cargo seemed to be almost entirely of fish they call here saumon blanc. They were sending up great baskets of them from the hold where they were very well packed in ice; half-way up they were thrown into a big tub which cleaned them—took off the salt and gave them a silvery look. They are put by hundreds into hand-carts which were waiting and carried off at once to the Halles. They had brought in 3,500 fish, but didn't seem to think they had made a very good haul. The whole cargo had been sold to a marieur and was sent off at once, by him, all over the country.

Other boats were also sending their cargo to the Halles. They had all kinds of fish—soles, mackerel, and a big red fish I didn't know at all. I wouldn't have believed, if I had not seen it with my own eyes, that such a bright-coloured fish could exist. However, a very sharp little boy, who was standing near and who answered all my questions, told me they were rougets. We went on to the Halles—a large gray stone building facing the sea—rather imposing with a square tower on top, from which one can see a long way out to sea and signal incoming fishing-boats. It was very clean—water running over the white marble slabs, and women, with pails and brushes, washing and wiping the floor. It is evidently a place that attracts strangers; many tourists were walking about—one couple, American, I think, passing through in an automobile and laying in a stock of lobsters and crabs (the big deep-sea crabs) and rougets. The man rather hesitated about leaving his auto in the streets; they had no chauffeur with them, tried to find a boy who would watch it. For a wonder none was forthcoming, but two young fishwives, who were standing near, said they would; when the man came back with his purchases he gave each of them a five-franc piece, which munificence so astounded them that they could hardly find words to thank him.

Quantities of fish of all kinds had arrived—some being sold à la criée, but it was impossible to understand the prices or the names of the fish—at least for us. The buying public seemed to know all about it. The fishwives were very busy standing behind the marble slabs with short thick knives, with which they cut off pieces of the large fish when the customer didn't want a whole one, and laughing and joking with every one. Here and there we saw a modern young person in a fancy blouse, her hair dressed and waved, with little combs, but there were not many. We bought some soles and shrimps. M. de G. tried to bargain a little for us, but the women were so smiling and so sure we didn't know anything about it, or what the current price of the fish was, that we had not much success.

The trawlers are gradually taking away all the trade from the old-fashioned fishing-boats. They go faster, carry more and larger nets, and are, of course, stronger sea-boats. They are not much more expensive. They burn coal of an inferior quality and their machinery is of the simplest description. There is not the loss of life with them that there must be always with the smaller sailing-boats.

Newfoundland is the most dangerous fishing ground, as the men have so much to contend with—the passing of transatlantic liners and the cold, thick fogs which come up off the banks—all of them prefer the Iceland fishing. The cold is greater, but there is much less fog and very few big boats to be met en route. Few of the Boulogne boats go to Newfoundland. It is generally the boats from Fécamp and some of the Breton ports that monopolize the fishing off the Banks. It seems that men often die from the cold and exposure in these waters. From the old-fashioned sailing-boats they usually send them off—two by two in a dory (they don't fish from the big boats); they start early, fish all day; if no fog comes up, they are all right and get back to their boats at dark, but if a sudden fog comes on they often can't find their boats and remain out all night, half frozen. *One* night they can stand, but *two* nights' cold and exposure are always fatal. When the fog lifts the little boat is sometimes quite close to the big one, but the men are dead—frozen. M. de G. tells us all sorts of terrible experiences that he has heard from his men, and yet they all like the life—wouldn't lead any other, and have the greatest contempt for a landsman.

There is a fruit stall at the corner of our street, where we stop every morning and buy fruit on our way down to the beach. We have become most intimate with the two women who are there. One, a young one with small children about the age of ours (to whom she often gives grapes or cherries when they pass), and the other a little, old, wrinkled, brown-faced grandmother, who sits all day, in all weathers, under an awning made of an old sail and helps her daughter. She has very bright eyes and looks as keen and businesslike as the young woman. She told us the other day she had *forty* grandchildren—all the males, men and boys, sailors and fishermen and "mousses"—many of the girls fishwives and the mothers married to fishermen or sailors. I asked her why some of them hadn't tried to do something else—there were so many things people could do in these days to earn their living without leading such a rough life. She was quite astonished at my suggestion—replied that they had lived on the sea all their lives and never thought of doing anything else. Her own husband had been a fisherman—belonged to one of the Iceland boats—went three or four times a year regularly—didn't come back one year—no tidings ever came of ship or crew—it was God's will, and when his time came he had to go, whether in his bed or on his boat. And she brought up all her sons to be sailors or fishermen, and when two were lost at sea, accepted that, too, as part of her lot, only said it was hard, sometimes, for the poor women when the winter storms came and the wind was howling and the waves thundering on the beach, and they thought of their men ("mon homme" she always called her husband when speaking of him), wet and cold, battling for their lives. I talked to her often and the words of the old song,

"But men must work and women must weep,
Though storms be sudden, and waters deep,
And the harbour bar be moaning,"

came back to me more than once, for the floating buoy at the end of the jetty makes a continuous dull melancholy sound when the sea is at all rough, and when it is foggy (the channel fogs come up very quickly) we hear fog horns all around us and quite distinctly the big sirène of Cap Gris Nez, which sends out its long wailing note over the sea. It is very powerful and is heard at a long distance.

The shops on the quay are an unfailing source of interest to me. I make a tour there every morning before I go down to the beach. They have such a wonderful variety of things. Shells of all sizes—enormous pink ones like those I always remember standing on the mantel-piece in the nursery at home—brought back by a sailor brother who used to tell us to put them to our ears and we would hear the noise of the sea—and beautiful delicate little mother-of-pearl shells that are almost jewels—wonderful frames, boxes, and pincushions, made of shells; big spoons, too, with a figure or a ship painted on them—knives, penholders, paper-cutters and brooches, made out of the bones of big fish—tassels of bright-coloured sea-weed, corals, vanilla beans—curiously worked leather belts—some roughly carved ivory crosses, umbrella handles, canes of every description, pipes, long gold earrings, parrots, little birds with bright-coloured feathers, monkeys—an extraordinary collection.

I am sure one would find many curious specimens if one could penetrate into the back of the old shops and pull the things about—evidently sailors from all parts of the world have passed at Boulogne. Still I don't hear many foreign languages spoken—almost always French and English; occasionally a dark face, with bright black eyes, strikes one. We saw two Italians the other day, talking and gesticulating hard, shivering, too, with woollen comforters tied over their caps. There was a cold fog and we were all wrapped up. It must be awful weather for Southerners who only live when the sun shines and go to bed when it is cold and gray. There are all sorts of itinerants, petits marchands, on the other side of the quay, looking on the water—old women with fruit and cakes—children with crabs and shrimps—dolls in Boulonaise costume—fishwives and matelottes, stalls with every description of food, tea, coffee, chocolate, sandwiches, and fried potatoes. The children bought some potatoes the other day wrapped up in brown paper—quite a big portion for two sous—and said they were very good.

The quais are very broad, happily, for everything is put there. One morning there were quantities of barrels. I asked what was in them. Salt, they told me, for the herring-boats which are starting these days. Nets, coils of ropes, big sails, baskets, boxes, odd bits of iron, some anchors—one has rather to pick one's way. An automobile has been standing there for three or four days. I asked if that was going to Iceland on a trawler, but the man answered quite simply, "Oh, no, Madame, what should we do with an automobile in a fishing-boat. It belongs to the owner of one of the ships, and has been here en panne waiting till he can have it repaired."

We went one evening to the Casino to see a "bal des matelottes." It was a curious sight—a band playing on a raised stand—a broad space cleared all round it and lots of people dancing. The great feature, of course, was the matelottes. Their costumes were very effective—they all wore short, very full skirts, different coloured jackets, short, with a belt, very good stout shoes and stockings, and their white frilled caps. They always danced together (very rarely with a man—it is not etiquette for them to dance with any man when their husbands or lovers are at sea), their hands on each other's shoulders. They dance perfectly well and keep excellent time and, I suppose, enjoy themselves, but they look very solemn going round and round until the music stops. Their feet and ankles are usually small. I heard an explanation the other day of their dark skins, clean cut features, and small feet. They are of Portuguese origin. The first foreign sailors who came to France were Portuguese. Many of them remained, married French girls, and that accounts for that peculiar type in their descendants which is very different from the look of the Frenchwoman in general. There are one or two villages in Brittany where the women have the same colouring and features, and there also Portuguese sailors had remained and married, and one still hears some Portuguese names—José, Manuel—and among the women some Annunziatas, Carmelas, etc. We had a house in Brittany one summer and our kitchen maid was called Dolores.

Cap Gris Nez.

We made a lovely excursion one day to Cap Gris Nez—just at the end of a wild bit of coast about twenty-five kilomètres from Boulogne. The road was enchanting on the top of the cliff all along the sea. We passed through Vimereux, a small bathing-place four or five miles from Boulogne, and one or two other villages, then went through a wild desolate tract of sand-hills and plains and came upon the lighthouse, one of the most important of the coast—a very powerful light that all inward-bound boats are delighted to see. There are one or two villas near on the top of the cliff, then the road turns sharply down to the beach—a beautiful broad expanse of yellow sand, reaching very far out that day as it was dead low tide.

In the distance we saw figures; couldn't distinguish what they were doing, but supposed they were fishing for shrimps, which was what our party meant to do. The auto was filled with nets, baskets, and clothes, as well as luncheon baskets. The hotel—a very good, simple one—with a broad piazza going all around it, was half-way down the cliff, and the woman was very "complaisante" and helpful—said there were plenty of shrimps, crabs, and lobsters and no one to fish. She and her husband had been out at four o'clock that morning and had brought back "quatre pintes" of shrimps. No one knew what she meant, but it was evidently a measure of some kind. I suppose an English pint. She gave us a cabin where the two young matrons dressed, or rather undressed, as they reappeared in their bathing trousers—which stopped some little distance above the knee—very short skirts, bare legs, "espadrilles" on their feet, and large Panama hats to protect them from the sun. The men had merely rolled up their trousers. They went out very far—I could just make them out—they seemed a part of the sea and sky, moving objects standing out against the horizon.

I made myself very comfortable with rugs and cushions under the cliff—I had my book as I knew it would be a long operation. It was enchanting—sitting there, such a beautiful afternoon. We saw the English coast quite distinctly. There was not a sound—no bathing cabins or tents, nobody on the shore, but a few fishermen were spreading nets on poles to catch the fish as the tide came up. The sea was quite blue, and as the afternoon lengthened there were lovely soft lights over everything; such warm tints it might almost have been the Mediterranean and the Riviera. A few fishing-boats passed in the distance, but there was nothing to break the great stillness—not even the ripple of the waves, as the sea was too far out. It was a curious sensation to be sitting there quite alone—the blue sea at my feet and the cliff rising straight up behind me.

The bay is small—two points jutting out on each side, completely shutting it in. There are a good many rocks—the water dashes over them finely when the tide is high and the sea rough. I got rather stiff sitting still and walked about a little on the hard beach and talked to the fishermen. They were looking on amused and indulgently at our amateurs, and said there were plenty of fish of all kinds *if* one knew how to take them. They said they made very good hauls with their nets in certain seasons—that lots of fish came in with the tide and got stranded, couldn't get back through the nets. One of them had two enormous crabs in his baskets, which I bought at once, and we brought them home in the bottom of the auto wrapped up in *very thick* paper, as they were still alive and could give a nasty pinch, the man said.

About five, I thought I made out my party more distinctly; their faces were turned homeward, so I went to meet them as far as the dry sand lasted. I had a very long walk as the tide was at its lowest. They came back very slowly, stopping at all the little pools and poking their nets under the rocks to get what they could. They had made a very fair basket of really big shrimps, were very wet, very hungry, and very pleased with their performance.

We had very good tea and excellent bread and butter at the hotel. They gave us a table on the piazza in the sun which finished drying the garments of the party. I fancy they had gone in deeper than they thought. However, salt water never gives cold and nobody was any the worse for the wetting. The woman of the hotel said we ought to go to see a fisherman's hut, on the top of the cliff near the lighthouse, before we went back. The same family of fishermen had lived there for generations, and it was a marvel how any one *could* live in such a place. We could find our way very easily as the path was marked by white stones. So we climbed up the cliff and a few minutes' walk brought us to one of the most wretched habitations I have ever seen: a little low stone hut, built so close to the edge of the cliff one would think a violent storm must blow it over—no windows—a primitive chimney, hardly more than a hole in the roof—a little low door that one had to stoop to pass through, one room, dark and cold—the floor of beaten earth, damp and uneven, almost in ruts. There were two beds, a table, two chairs, and a stove—nondescript garments hanging on the walls—a woman with a baby was sitting at the table—another child on the floor—both miserable little, puny, weak-eyed, pale children. The woman told me she had six—all lived there—one man was sitting on the bed mending a net, another on the floor drinking some black stuff out of a cup—I think the baby was drinking the same—two or three children were stretching big nets on the top of the cliff—they, too, looked miserable little specimens of humanity, bare-legged, unkempt, trousers and jackets in holes; however, the woman was quite cheerful—didn't complain nor ask for money. The men accepted two francs to drink our health. One wonders how children ever grow up in such an atmosphere without light or air or decent food.

The drive home was beautiful—not nearly so lonely. Peasants and fishermen were coming back from their work—women and children driving the cows home. We noticed, too, a few little, low, whitewashed cottages in the fields, almost hidden by the sand-hills, which we hadn't seen coming out.

HARDELOT.

Hardelot was a great resource to us. It is a fine domain, beautiful pine woods running down to the sea—a great stretch of green meadow and a most picturesque old castle quite the type of the château-fort. The castle has now been transformed into a country club with golf-links, tennis, and well-kept lawns under big trees which give a splendid shade and are most resting to the eye after the glare of the beach. There is no view of the sea from the castle, but from the top of the towers on a fine day one just sees a quiver of light beneath the sky-line which might be the sea.

The château has had its history like all the old feudal castles on the sea-board and has changed hands very often, being sometimes French and sometimes English. It was strongly fortified and resisted many attacks from the English before it actually came into their possession. Part of the wall and a curious old gate-way are all that remain of the feudal days. The castle is said to have been built by Charlemagne. Henry VIII of England lived in it for some time, and the preliminaries of a treaty of peace between that monarch and François I were signed there—the French and English ambassadors arriving in great state—with an endless army of retainers. One wonders where they all were lodged, as the castle could never have been large—one sees that from the foundations; but I fancy habits were very simple in those days, and the suites probably slept on the floor in one of the halls with all their clothes on, the troopers keeping on their jack-boots so long that they had to be cut off sometimes—the feet and legs so swollen.

The drive from the club to the plage is charming. Sometimes through pretty narrow roads with high banks on each side, with hedges on top, quite like parts of Devonshire, and nice, little, low, whitewashed cottages with green shutters and red doors, much more like England than France.

We stopped at a cottage called the Dickens House, where Charles Dickens lived for some time. It is only one story high—white with green shutters—stands at the end of an old-fashioned garden filled with all sorts of ordinary garden-flowers—roses, hollyhocks, larkspurs, pinks, all growing most luxuriantly and making patches of colour in the green surroundings. We saw Dickens' study, his table still in the window (where he always wrote), looking over the garden to an endless stretch of green fields.

The plage is very *new*. There is a nice clean hotel, with broad piazzas and balconies directly on the sea and a few chalets are already built, but there is an absolute dearth of trees and shade. There was quite a strong sea-breeze the day we were there, and the fine white sand was blown high into the air in circles, getting into our eyes and hair. There is a splendid beach—miles of sand—not a rock or cliff—absolutely level. The domain of Hardelot belongs to a company of which Mr. John Whitley was the president. He had concessions for a tramway from Boulogne to Hardelot which will certainly bring people to the plage and club. Now there is only an auto-bus, which goes very slowly and is constantly out of order; once the club is organized, I think it cannot fail to be a charming resort. There is plenty of game in the forest (they have a good piece of it), perfect golf and tennis grounds—as much deep-sea fishing as one wants. We went often to tea at the château. F. played golf, and we walked about and sat under the trees, and the children were quite happy playing on the lawns where they were as safe as in their nurseries.

Lector House believes that a society develops through a two-fold approach of continuous learning and adaptation, which is derived from the study of classic literary works spread across the historic timeline of literature records. Therefore, we aim at reviving, repairing and redeveloping all those inaccessible or damaged but historically as well as culturally important literature across subjects so that the future generations may have an opportunity to study and learn from past works to embark upon a journey of creating a better future.

This book is a result of an effort made by Lector House towards making a contribution to the preservation and repair of original ancient works which might hold historical significance to the approach of continuous learning across subjects.

HAPPY READING & LEARNING!

LECTOR HOUSE LLP
E-MAIL: info@lectorhouse.com

9 789356 147041

Printed by Libri Plureos GmbH in Hamburg,
Germany